Rosa May:
The Search for A
Mining Camp Legend

2nd Revised Edition

by George Williams III

D0061955

Tree By The River Publishing Trust (Psalm 1)
P.O. Box 20703
Carson City, Nevada 89721
www.autographed-books.com
1-775-750-8646

Rosa May: The Search for a Mining Camp Legend
2nd Revised Edition
By George Williams III

Published by:
Tree By The River Publishing Trust
P.O. Box 20703
Carson City, Nevada 89721
To order books go to www.autographed-books.com

Other non-fiction books by George Williams III:

Mark Twain: His Life In Virginia City, Nevada
Mark Twain: His Adventures at Aurora and Mono Lake
Mark Twain and the Jumping Frog of Calaveras County
Rosa May: The Search For A Mining Camp Legend
The Guide to Bodie and Eastern Sierra Historic Sites
The Redlight Ladies of Virginia City, Nevada
The Murders at Convict Lake
The Songwriter's Demo Manual and Success Guide
Eastern Sierra Hot Springs
In the Last of the Wild West
Nevada Hot Springs
Hot Springs of Northern California
Repair Your Credit

Copyright 2012   Tree By The River Publishing Trust

For Edie,
without whose love,
belief and encouragement,
this book could not have been written.
Thank you.

*Like as a father pitieth his children, so the Lord
    pitieth them that fear him.
For he knoweth our frame; he remembereth that
    we are dust.
As for man, his days are as grass; as a flower of the field,
    so he flourisheth.
For the wind passeth over it, and it is gone; and the place
    thereof shall know it no more.
But the mercy of the Lord is from everlasting to
        everlasting upon them that fear him, and
        his righteousness unto children's children,
To such as keep his covenant
And to those who remember His
        commandments to do them.*

Psalm 103:13-17 King James

4

Chapter 1

If you ever come to the ghost town of Bodie, California, you will find her as I found her. She is buried in the outcast cemetery just beyond the barbed wire fence. Someone cut the last rung of wire in the fence near her grave and there is a hole there now. Thousands of visitors crawl through the hole to reach her grave. The dirt about her grave has been beaten bare by many who want to know who this is, buried in the outcast cemetery.

Her peculiar gravestone stands far from others with none to keep it company. The base is a rectangular slab of concrete. Standing on this is cemented another concrete slab, several inches narrower in width and slightly curved at the top. The top portion of this slab was meant to be a smooth, evenly cut curve as with some of the finer stones in the cemetery above. But this craftsman, lacking skill or the proper tools, cut a jagged curve and the top portion is oddly lopsided. The standing slab is painted white and with its lopsided top resembles an ice cream cone that has slowly melted. Hard mountain weather has blasted the paint away in patches and the raw concrete shows through. It is surprising that any paint remains on her marker after all these years.

With her gravestone in such ragged condition it seems certain remaining family members no longer live nearby. If so, they would have whitened her marker long ago.

The letters of her name were carved into the marker when the concrete was soft and pliable. The printed letters are contorted and child-like. Printed is her first name, and, below, what sounds like her middle name. The marker appears to be without the woman's birth and death years. But if you stoop down and carefully examine the stone "1880" is faintly scribbled.

One takes 1880 as the year she died. Yet the date is so faintly scribbled, one wonders whether or not the stone maker was certain himself of the woman's time of death.

A red cross is carved deep and wide into the concrete above her name. The blood red cross of Christ burns brightly against the white marker like a blessing.

At the base of the gravestone where the two slabs are cemented together, there is an imprint of a tiny shoe. One feels that the shoe must have belonged to the woman buried beneath. Still, the shoe imprint seems strange.

Beside the shoe imprint are two words: "by Serventi." The name is obviously Italian. Was this woman Italian? Was Serventi her husband, her brother or a lover? Or was Serventi the Bodie undertaker? Perhaps Serventi was a friend who made the poor woman this marker out of kindness. Though his tribute is lopsided and unprofessional, the marker's flaws make her seem more human, more worthy of pity.

Whoever Serventi was and whatever she was to him, he had cared enough for the woman to haul this three hundred pound stone up the hill to mark her otherwise anonymous grave.

Those who find her gravestone outside the fence believe she is buried beneath it. They do not know that her gravestone was made years after her death and placed here by a man who never knew her nor exactly where she is buried. He unknowingly placed her gravestone one hundred and fifty feet from where she is actually buried.

Long ago when she was buried, a square wood fence was placed around her grave. Those who supposedly loved her made the fence but did not make a headstone with her name, birth and death years. Only the anonymous fence. Each side of the fence was square and two boards ran crisscross, making each side look like a square with an X inside. That is how her outcast grave looked long ago before someone tore the fence down. With the fence gone, there was nothing left to mark her grave. Sagebrush moved in and swallowed the mound of earth as if to hide her grave from any who might seek to find it.

It took a long time of searching before I found an early photograph of the Bodie cemetery that shows exactly where her grave is. The photo was taken in 1927 and shows the entire Bodie cemetery and various landmarks in the town beyond. Her crisscross fence stands far from other marked graves, by itself in the outcast cemetery.

I took that photo and had an 8x10 and a 5x8 copy made.

Photos in hand, I searched the lower slopes of the outcast cemetery for her grave. I found many graves in a forest of sagebrush. It was difficult to determine which was hers.

Using landmarks in the 1927 photo of the Bodie cemetery I finally located her grave after several days of careful searching. It was so thickly overrun with sagebrush that I had to chop it down with an axe. After I cleared the sagebrush away, I piled stones on her tiny mound so that the grave would not be lost again. Locating her grave was somewhat of a victory for me. It had taken three obsessed years to learn her story and locate her actual grave. In that time of labored searching, we had become friends in a strange sort of way.

When she was very young, her dreams were beat out of her by a stern man and woman who lacked imagination and intelligence. They were unhappy that life had brought them so little. They had given up dreaming long ago. It was foolishness. Whenever they looked at their pretty and intelligent daughter and saw how her eyes glistened, how they hoped and dreamed, they became angry with her. They scolded and criticized her needlessly until the dullness in their eyes began to grow in hers. They made her believe that anything as worthless as she could never have the dreams she dreamed. She became angry with her parents and inwardly angry at herself. Someday she would make them suffer the pain she had endured all those years while living with them.

The sternness and lack of imagination of her father and mother eventually broke her faith in herself and in her future. She was headed for a terrible tragedy. Still her soul longed for Freedom—freedom from her parent's abuse and freedom from something she did not understand. Someday when she was old enough she would leave her parents, go far away and never come back.

She came West to Virginia City, Nevada in the mid-1870's when that mining camp was full of silver and freedom seekers like herself. She was just another pretty thing that ended up on "the line." For nearly twenty years she wasted her youth in Virginia City and Carson City whorehouses. One morning in 1892 she awoke to discover she was thirty-seven.

Thirty-seven. She was too old now for the high-class brothels. She was no longer the attractive young girl she once was. She had never looked far enough into the future to see herself growing old and losing her beauty and appeal. The rosy color of youth was gone from her cheeks. She needed more of the pink powder fluffed on her face to compete with the young girls who were taking her place and making the kind of money she once made.

In the mirror she saw the lines that cracked about her mouth and spread from her eyes like sullen rays of doom. And yes, she had to admit, she had put on some weight. Her arms were fleshy; her thighs and butt were thicker; there was more weight in her face. Her being so stout made it all the more apparent. But now there was something in her eyes that had not been there before. It was a cold, steely hardness. It had come from too many years of too many men. It had come from too many years of hustling, too many years of scrounging from one whorehouse to the next, too long a time of reckless living. It had all caught up with her at last. Certainly part of "the life" had been fun; but the fun was gone out of it. Now the hardness was in her eyes and it would not go away. The customers saw it and it made them not want to go up the stairs with her. She knew men liked the young stuff. Why hadn't she seen this moment coming?

It didn't matter. The madams had. They had kept her on too long as it was. They had fed her, clothed her, and taken care of her when she was young and still had something to offer. Now her youth was gone and her beauty was fading. They put her out in the streets.

For years she had known the security of the madam telling her what was right and wrong. Now that substitute parent was gone. As she stood on the darkening street, the biting winter wind crawled up the sleeves of her coat. The sudden, shattering loneliness crept into her stomach. She couldn't shake it off. She couldn't believe after all these years it could come to this.

She looked through her past searching for someone to

run to, someone to save her. She remembered Ernie, Ernest Marks. She had loved Marks long ago when they were young, but he did her dirt like the rest; she always made them do her dirt. But at times he had been good to her. Marks ran a saloon in Bodie now; it was called the Laurel Palace. She knew Bodie wasn't the mining camp it used to be but that might be a good reason to go there.

The gold camp of Bodie had boomed in 1879 just as Virginia City began to decline. The greedy opportunists knew Virginia City had few years of prosperity left and struck out for the new camp.

From 1879 until 1882 Bodie saw high times. Gold was plentiful and men and women were eager to get to Bodie. As with all mining camps, Bodie's boom collapsed when production of high grade ore declined. Of Bodie's population of ten thousand, eight thousand deserted Bodie pronto. They headed for the Colorado strikes and other new and promising camps.

About two thousand stayed on, mostly miners and their families. Bodie settled down to a regular small town of white frame cottages with mining its one and only industry.

The camp would have died in the 1890's if the cyanide process had not been discovered and introduced into the Bodie mining facilities. This new process of gold extraction gave Bodie a new lease on life. With the cyanide process the camp was able to support a population of about fifteen hundred. Most of those who stayed believed Bodie would one day boom again. Always after the fall, there remained those who believed the boom camp would rise again. Few ever did.

About 1892, at the age of thirty-seven, she came to Bodie. Bodie was no longer the boom camp it once was, and she no longer the woman she had been. The dying mining camp of Bodie was ideal. There would be less competition here. The smart young whores went to the boom camps.

She moved into a little white house on Bonanza Street in Chinatown, the low part of town on the north end. Here for twenty more years she introduced young Bodie males to sex. She comforted the lonely butcher whose wife thought sex too

9

dirty or too inconvenient. She held her door open for the ugly misfits no woman would have, and gave the middle-aged man his last fling before the long decline. She took on chinks and blacks, whites and Indians, farmer, lawyer, banker, miner, rancher, cowboy; high and low; big and small, anyone with a buck. And all the time she drank more because the dying light in her reminded her morning after sleepless morning that it had all been a waste. She had not made the world pay for her pain. She was growing old and she was not loved. The overwhelming sadness haunted her.

There were women in Bodie who hated her. Their stinging eyes followed her when she came uptown to browse in the shops. She had put up with the angry eyes of such women for so long that their staring no longer bothered her. And this only made the women who hated her more angry. But it galled them to see their sons and daughters waiting in the streets for the woman from Chinatown. The children all knew the dark haired woman from Chinatown handed out dimes as if the silver coins were birdseed. And a dime for any Bodie child was a great meal ticket to Cecil Burkham's candy counter.

Though she troubled some of Bodie's women, the men did not think twice about her. In their time, her kind were taken for granted. Such women were little gifts from God, fathers brought their virgin sons to, lonely men went for temporary comfort and middle-aged men went to reaffirm their manhood. Certainly she wasn't the kind of girl you brought home to Mom. She was simply a fact of life and useful sometimes. So the men did not run her out of town. In fact, the money they paid her provided her with a means of living and gave her a niche in their community. Though she was as much a part of their town as the blacksmith or the butcher, few would have admitted so.

One November when the snow was deep and the gray sky shivered, and the acid wind ripped across the barren hills, her few friends dragged her corpse out of town on a sled. She had not died a happy death. The handful of Bodie women who hated her finally had their revenge. They put up a huge fuss and would not allow her to be buried among the decent folk in the higher cemetery. The men who lived in Bodie and had been her clients for over twenty years did not speak up to defend her. They did not want to hurt or embarrass their families. Her friends were forced to bury her on the lower slopes of the cemetery outside the fence. As the cold wind tore across their faces and blew snow in their eyes, it was not easy to break the frozen earth with their pickaxes.

She had always loved the mountains. She felt protected by the huge mounds of earth and stone surrounding her. The mountains were like fortresses safeguarding her from the outside world. And as if to please her, two of the most famous mining camps ever—Virginia City and Bodie—sprang up at the foot of mountains surrounded by other mountains.

In Virginia City, she had lived many years beneath towering Sun Mountain. Each day as the sun slid behind the mountain and the mountain's shadow crept over Virginia City, she began her workday. Her workday ended with the first light creeping over the mountains east of town.

In Bodie, her tiny white cottage lay at the foot of Bodie Bluff, the barren, sage-ridden mountain, where men climbed and dug out the gold. Here, as in Virginia and Carson City, the town was encompassed by the barren Bodie Hills and they had made her feel protected.

Bodie was by far the most rugged and isolated mining camp she had lived in. At 8,372 feet, winter came early and lasted a good eight months. With winter came the fierce cold and the snow that nearly covered the houses in snowdrifts, cutting the camp off from the outside world. Only the heartiest efforts got a man in and out. Bridgeport, the nearest town, was twenty miles away and it took the man who carried the mail by horse and sled, one full day to make the trip from Bridgeport to Bodie.

To the north and down Bodie Canyon, there was Aurora, seventeen miles away. Aurora was another mining camp and as isolated as Bodie. There were train connections to Carson City at Hawthome, Nevada, thirty-six miles away, but Hawthorne was even more difficult to reach than Bridgeport.

She had not minded the isolation. She had come to Bodie

because of the isolation and it was the isolation that kept her there so long. As the years slipped by she had grown to need the isolation more and more. For with the years, truth had become I more deadly. Truth, which had always chased her like a dog chasing his tail, had caught up with her with age despite Bodie's isolation.

The Bodie Hills have changed little in the millions of years since volcanoes erupted and spewed lava in all directions forming the Hills and leaving them covered with basalt forever. The deep brown and burned basalt is often canyon walls high or strewn about the Hills in huge chunks, in places making the land look more like a lunar surface than earth. The barren, basalt Hills are as lonesome and as wild as ever and for the majority of their existence man has had little to do with them. There were the Piutes who trotted through them during summer and collected pinon nuts in the fall. And there were the white men who roamed and mined in the Hills from the 1850s on after Aurora boomed.

But for the most part, men have left the Hills alone. Men had little to do with them before gold was discovered and have little to do with them now that the gold is gone.

The Bodie Hills lie east of the Sierra, south of Bridgeport Valley and north of Mono Lake, a monstrous sea of brackish water fed by the Sierra runoff and surrounding hills. Sagebrush grows hip high and there is much rabbit brush, yellow flowered when blooming. The foothills are pea green colored from the sagebrush and the slivers of grass that grow in the sandy soil between the sage and basalt. Dark green, cone shaped pinon pines dot the lower foothills. But as the Hills rise in elevation, there are fewer pinon pines and the sagebrush no longer grows hip high. In order to survive the severe cold and wind in the higher Hills, the sagebrush has cropped itself and grows in stout bushes.

In summer, the higher Hills are green from the sagebrush. In a few canyons where water collects, stands of aspens, small and twisted by the snow and wind, struggle for survival. The pinon pines do not grow in the higher Hills and but for the few canyons of aspens, the Hills are barren of trees.

In the spring as the snow melts the black earth returns in patches. The wind blows the remaining snow into huge white strips and the Hills are zebra marked. Patches of snow stay on the Hills through mid-summer where the snow has piled in drifts. Though summer days are warm enough for a man to go bare chested, nights can freeze standing water.

In the spring the melted snow curls down the canyons in skinny creeks and drains into the flat places between hills and the grass is thick and moist in the flat places. There are springs too, in the mouths of canyons and the spring water is very good and cold. Small animals— rabbits, chipmunks, ground squirrels and deer drink at the springs and feed on the lush grass beside the water.

By mid-summer, the Hills are beautiful with wild flowers, fields of blue and white lupine, red Indian Paintbrush, wild daisies, irises and the fried-egg flowers- all white with a large yellow center.

In summer the sky is wide and blue with huge islands of cumulus clouds. The air smells very fresh and wild, mostly from the rich pungent smell of the white sagebrush. Depending on the summer, between every five days and two weeks, the cumulus clouds gather into black thunderheads and storm the Hills. The storms are brief, for an hour or so but the rain falls full and hard. Afterward the Hills smell wonderful with the damp, wild smell of the wet sage. It is an unmistakably fresh fragrance you easily fall in love with and miss when you are away from.

By September, nights in the Bodie Hills have grown bitterly cold. By October the long hard winter has set in. In a short time the snow comes and the green, sage covered Hills become white until the June warmth returns.

In the narrow valley below her grave, what remains of the boom camp she knew stands for all who care to see it. The wood frame buildings are brown and cracked from so many hard winters. The years have stripped their paint coverings. They stand naked to the wind, cold and heat. Their elderly sides lean in, roofs are caving in, windows are cracked or missing. Outhouses have fallen and rot where they lay. Heaps of tin and broken glass are scattered through the dead settlement. Model T's rust in the fields.

Wooden wagons stand unattended. Cattle gather in empty lots where houses and saloons once stood. They leave their droppings behind without shame.

In the early morning and evenings or at intervals during the day when visitors have packed up and crawled back to the highway, it is then that you come to know Bodie best and learn why places like this are called ghost towns. The streets are naked of concrete and tar, naked too of the people who lived beside them and walked them day after day. They are gone now, it is still and lonely. A slight wind comes up. The saloons are dusty and empty; the cottages are without miners and their families; their church is without worshipers; their school house empty of children's noises; their giggles, shouts and whimpers, all gone.

Bodie Bluff, the steep hill just east of town, is without the beehive of miners and wagons that once crawled over the mountain seeking its golden honey. The huge mound of dirt and rock is pitted and gouged where men dug for gold. The mountain looks ravaged as if some beast dug into its sides and tore from its depths something vital and necessary for survival. There are piles of rock and golden sand beside the beast's holes. From one hole to the next are paths, mere lines from a distance. The paths are no longer traveled nor are the holes and piles of rock bothered with any longer. The people who lived here have no use for Bodie Bluff now that the gold has been harvested. They have deserted the mountain and their houses. They are gone.

As you walk up deserted Main Street, you pass the Miner's Union Hall. For years it has missed the clomp of miner's boots. Farther down, there is Harvey Boone's general store with its elaborate door and window moldings. They speak of a more extravagant era. There is a barber's shop without customers, a stable without horses or blacksmith, a Chinese washhouse, an assay office.

But it is the Standard Mill that is most obvious. The mill is enclosed in gray corrugated steel. Several windows are broken out. Three rusting smoke stacks stick out of the roof like long fingers reaching for the sky. There is a rusted flag pole where the patriotic once raised the flag. Strewn about the Standard are assorted discarded mining machinery: a rusting engine, rusting iron pipe, the squashed body of an early car. Long ago the pounding of the Standard was heard day and night at any part of town. Its thunder filled the tiny valley and reached out for several miles. The people of Bodie did not mind the incessant pounding. The Standard was the heart of their community. They wondered and feared whenever its roaring ceased. The pounding only stopped when the machinery broke down or when the pipes froze in winter. Otherwise, the mill ran continually, pounding tons of gold-quartz into powder, assuring the people that the ore from Bodie Bluff would last forever.

At the end of north Main Street there are piles of waste rock from the mines. The gold and red rock is now the home of various little animals. A chipmunk scurries over the rocks. A ground squirrel stands poised until you come too near. Then he squeaks his warning cry and dashes for his home.

In empty lots, roaming cattle munch the moist grass. A cow moos for her stray calf. The calf comes running to her. He plunges his head into her milk sack and sucks her brown udders.

Across town a lone bull calls to his herd. He haws and haws until they follow him up a canyon. The bull's hawing echoes through the still valley. Blackbirds follow the cattle, the glistening black feathers of the male birds, the dull gray feathers of females, their click-click bird talk can be heard. Flies buzz in your ear and about the piles of fresh manure.

You walk into the sage covered lots behind Main Street. There are rows of tiny cottages here. The sagebrush grows thick and high beside them. It grows thicker every year as if it longs to topple the houses. The roofs of the cottages are covered with squares of tin cut from large containers and tacked to the roof to keep out rain and snow. A loose piece rattles in the wind.

Lots beside the houses are strewn with more rubbish, rusting tin, broken windows, heaps of green and violet glass, busted pipe, scattered chunks of brick, foundations of buildings that have long burned down, holes where outhouses once stood and large round holes where water was hauled out in buckets. The wells are filled now with rocks, timber and trash. They are useless.

As the summer sun dips toward the western hills, shadows curl about the buildings and streets. The air turns chilly. You watch the barn swallows as they flutter up to their mud nests beneath the roof of the assay office. You see the tiny baby birds open their yellow mouths as the parent birds steadily flutter, dunking food into the eager mouths.

You walk up Main Street and you imagine the world that once lived on this street long ago. The clomp and snorting of horses is gone. The shouting of boys off to baseball games is gone. The rattling wagons, the pounding of the stage, the giggles of adolescent girls, the heated talk of miners and speculators, the searing language of whores, gamblers and drunks, all gone.

Chapter 2

It's hard to believe three years have passed since I first visited Bodie and stumbled on Rosa May's grave. I had no idea that July day I would spend the next three years researching and chronicling the life of one of Bodie's legends. The last thing on my mind was setting about researching anything, never mind writing a book. I had had my fill of books and research papers.

I was another tourist, one of thousands who each year bump their way over the dirt roads for a glimpse of the old West. Like others before me, I discovered Rosa May's legend told in books and local yarns: the story of a good hearted prostitute who died one winter long ago while nursing miners through a pneumonia epidemic. Despite her valiant efforts to save lives, Rosa May was denied burial in the cemetery.

The injustice of Rosa May's story disturbs many today. Burying kind hearted Rosa May outside the fence, seems cruel. Yet in Rosa's era, such ostracism was common.

Rosa May's story reminded me of the adulteress who was dragged before Jesus by an angry mob who was about to stone her. According to the law of Moses, they were commanded to stone her to death. Jesus turned from the mob as if he had not heard them. He knelt and wrote with a finger in the sand. One wonders whether he wrote each man's name and a few of the sins they had committed.

As they continued to pressure him, Jesus stood and said: "He that is without sin among you, let him first cast a stone at her." Convicted by their own consciences, one by one, beginning with the eldest, the men walked away.

Left alone with the woman, Jesus said to her, "Woman, where are your accusers? Has no man condemned you?"

"No man, Lord."

"Neither do I condemn you: go and sin no more."

It's a touching story. If each of us could be as forgiving. Today Rosa May's outcast grave reminds us that once, long ago, there was an unforgiving people, who, like Rosa, have passed on.

During my research I found many who hold Rosa May's story dear. Many identify with her injustice. The reason is simple: each of us has at some time been treated unjustly. We seldom forget such experiences or those responsible.

Rosa May's outcast grave represents to these, the part of them that has experienced injustice. They feel sympathy for Rosa May because they have shared similar experiences. Because they feel a part of her, they are able to have compassion for her. Many of these, like myself, want to know who was Rosa May? Why did she become a prostitute? Where did she come from? What was her life really like? Is there any truth to her legend?

For the thousands who have come to Bodie and asked these questions there have never been any real answers until now.

In the past three years I have traveled twenty thousand miles by car with little money; scoured every relevant city, county, state, national and church record; scrutinized hundreds of photographs; devoured sixty books, numerous articles and forty years of newspapers; wrote one hundred and sixty research letters; interviewed every one of Bodie's survivors; spent hundreds of hours in museums, libraries and courthouses, thousands of hours piecing her life together.

It has been worth it. I have uncovered some answers to Rosa May's curious life. I believe I understand why Rosa May became a prostitute.

This is the story of how I unearthed Rosa May's life from gossip, myth and fact.

Chapter 3

Three summers ago, Kevin Lamb and I were hired as entertainers at Mammoth Lakes, California, a popular ski resort three hundred miles north of Los Angeles, high in the Eastern Sierra. During our stay at Mammoth Lakes I visited nearby Bodie and became interested in the legend of Rosa May.

Surrounded by mountains and wilderness, Mammoth Lakes prospers all year. In the higher country above the resort are the series of green lakes from which Mammoth Lakes takes its name. The lakes are in steps, each slightly higher in elevation than the next. When spring comes, the warm weather drives the melted snow down from the high peaks through steep canyons into the lakes. The water flows freely from the higher lakes to the lower lakes and finally down a rocky canyon through the forest and resort. Mammoth Creek, as it is then called, provides fine trout fishing when the water warms. The Creek waters the valley, feeding the moist green plants and wild flowers that thrive beside its sweet waters.

During the 1870's and 80's, men searched Mammoth Creek and the mountains for gold. They found gold in what is known today as Old Mammoth. Here, for a time, the small mining camp of Mammoth Lakes prospered. But unlike her more fortunate neighbor, Bodie, Mammoth's gold was soon exhausted and the frustrated treasure hunters left the Creek and the lakes. They left behind several log cabins and a rusting mill in Old Mammoth.

Today Mammoth Lakes is a gold mine of another sort. Immediately after the first good snow, thousands of skiers swarm into the little mountain town. The skiers are mostly from the Los Angeles area, a good six hour drive away. They are the resort's principal income.

Arriving Friday, wearing brightly colored wool knit caps, mirrored sun glasses and nylon jackets, the skiers quickly fill the motels and condominiums. Rushing to the slopes of Mammoth Mountain, they wait in long lines at the lifts, and afterward, long lines at the restaurants.

Sunday, bone weary from several days of skiing and partying, they mount their skis to the roofs of their cars. All day and late into the night, cars with fogged-up windows, bumper to bumper, begin the long drive back to LA, their passengers glad to have gotten away a day or two.

Winter is Mammoth's most profitable season. Summer still draws many vacationers to fish and camp in the mountains. It was in June that Kevin and I first went to Mammoth for a four week gig at Whisky Creek, perhaps the most popular of Mammoth's dinner houses.

Back in Riverside, California, we had just finished six months at another club. In the past five years we had played many of the bars and clubs in the Riverside-San Bernardino area. We had become seasoned musicians and entertainers.

Ironically, what brought me to Mammoth that summer, and what eventually led to the search for Rosa May, was a dream I had had for nearly twenty years: the dream of writing songs and performing them before audiences. That dream had taken a lot of hard, disciplined work, but it had given back some wonderful moments.

It began when I was a kid, when my parents and I visited my grandmother. She had a crippled, old piano. Many of the ivories were missing or cigarette scarred, and the finish was cracked and wrinkled like an old man's face. And, it was terribly out of tune. I tinkered with that piano each time we visited my grandmother. I learned to play simple songs by ear. I recall how I used red nail polish to mark the white keys to remember where each song started. The white keys looked awful with the red nail polish, but no one cared. It was an old piano.

When I was thirteen, my urge for musical expression suddenly reemerged while listening to Sandy Nelson's, "LET THERE BE DRUMS," a record composed mainly of pounding African rhythms. I wanted to play the drums like Sandy Nelson.

Inspired, I visited the local music store. I drooled over the glittering red drums displayed in the window. But my hopes fell when caught the price tag. I would never be a drummer.

20

Instead, I bought a second-hand guitar, and learned to play by ear and watching other guitar players on stage.

At fourteen I was playing lead guitar in a group and making money. I began writing songs. I played in groups and continued writing music through high school.

For a hyperactive only child, whose home was not happy, music was an answer. It helped combat low self-esteem caused in large part by my father who was very critical, at times cruel and distant. Music also helped assuage the pain of my parents marital troubles. And it helped me survive the crushing experience of seeing my mother crumble before me.

My mother as a child had a home life that was a horror story. Her father was an alcoholic who beat my mother, her brothers and sisters, and kept them awake at night as he howled and pounded walls. There were nights my mother and her sister lay newspaper on the bedroom floor for a place to urinate. They would not dare venture to the bathroom for fear of being beaten. There were dinner times their father threw their plates full of food to the floor, Christmases he destroyed their gifts without reason or provocation, times he beat their mother in front of them.

My mother had her first nervous breakdown at fourteen, her second at sixteen. The emotional wounds never healed. My mother was a sensitive, deep feeling person who needed tremendous love and understanding.

When I was sixteen, severe depression caused my mother to sleep eighteen hours a day. My father, who was distracted by his own emotional problems, never sought medical help. My mother eventually cracked-up. My father left her.

Music helped me get through it. It helped me make friends and brought me attention. It helped me express my anger and hurt. And it gave me hope. Somewhere down the road was stardom, and with it I foolishly thought, was happiness, stability and the reassurance I wanted.

I studied music in college for several years, dropped out, and returned to study literature to improve my lyric writing. While in college I continued performing in concerts, coffee houses, bars and on radio.

After I graduated as an English major, I sang in bars full

time. As a bar musician and entertainer, my job was to draw people in, talk it up during breaks, keep customers happy and keep them drinking. It had little to do with making music. Sometimes it made you feel like a prostitute. But at the time it was one way a singer/songwriter could make a living, until he was well known and drew people to concerts.

My good friend Kevin Lamb and I had teamed up as a duo. We had managed to interest record producers and we were about to record an album after the gig at Mammoth. At twenty-six, it seemed my dream of becoming a successful singer/ songwriter was about to come true.

Chapter 4

Our engagement at Whisky Creek was going well. We worked five nights a week, Wednesday through Sunday, 8:30 to 1:30 A.M. The best nights were Friday through Sunday because of the weekend crowds. Many in our audience were on vacation, happy to be free of their humdrum routines. People were feeling good and in a mood to be entertained which made our work easier and more enjoyable. The Whisky Creek audience was the best we had had while working bars. Mammoth, being a resort, had a lot to do with people loosening up. Having audiences that most often listened, applauded and joked with us raised our confidence and revived our spirits. We tried to give our audiences what they were giving us.

The engagement apparently went well enough that we were asked to stay on through July. This meant another month of work and time to hike and explore the region. If we had not been hired for July, I most likely would have never visited Bodie and discovered Rosa May's grave.

The first week of July, we drove up to Lake Tahoe to catch a show at a casino. On the way up Highway 395 I spotted the road sign for Bodie. I had never been to a ghost town. I made a mental note to visit Bodie before we left Mammoth.

About a week later I made the hour and a half drive from Mammoth to Bodie. To be specific, the day was July 8, because July 9 is written on the rough draft of the lyrics for "Rosa May." The song had nearly written itself the following morning after my trip to Bodie. I awoke with the tune in my head, and finished the music in fifteen minutes. The lyrics took a couple hours. I thought it was strange how easily the song came, and frankly, it sort of spooked me.

The day before, I had joggled down the Cottonwood Canyon dirt road north of Mono Lake into Bodie. I traveled on the road a hundred years earlier, thousands of gold hungry men and women had traveled over. Only they had not ventured to

Bodie in a '67 VW Bug, but in thrashing stage coaches, rattling steel wheeled wagons, by horse and foot.

I parked in the parking lot near the Bodie Cemetery. Old cemeteries fascinate me. The first place I visited was the Bodie cemetery.

I noticed that many of the pine markers did not have the names and dates of those buried beneath. The hard Bodie weather had blasted away the carved and painted letters. Many graves were overrun with sagebrush which had toppled the encircling fences.

As I left the cemetery, I noticed a lone white marker with its back to me. Curious, I crawled under the barbed wire fence. The marker was Rosa May's. It seemed odd that there were no other markers near hers. Strange, too, that her marker was without birth and death years. I stood by her grave for a time, and wondered who she was and why she was buried out here by herself.

The thought came to me that her rugged, lonely marker could be used in a song about Bodie.

I walked down the hill from the cemetery through the sagebrush. I crossed the perimeter road and went through a field where tin cans and glass were strewn about and wagons stood unattended.

Along with other tourists I made the self-guided tour through the ghost town, peeking in windows, fascinated. Bodie was once the kind of wild mining town portrayed in hundreds of westerns. Like others, I wished I had lived a hundred years earlier and known Bodie when it was the roaring boom camp, filled with frenzied men and women, saloons that roared day and night, and fools who battled each other with six-guns.

In the Bodie Museum I learned Rosa May had been a prostitute. That was why she was buried in the outcast cemetery. As someone who rooted for losers, I was immediately curious.

In a glass display case I found a small black lantern with red glass windows: "Rosa May's Red Light." Beside the lantern were various pieces of Victorian clothing, and a framed photograph of Rosa May, a pretty girl of about nineteen, with short, dark, curly hair. She was sitting, dressed in a black Victorian gown with long sleeves. There was white lace around the cuffs and the collar of her dress. She sat with her left hand in her lap with a bracelet around her left wrist. Her right hand curled up toward her neck, and the delicate fingers held a thin chain that swung from a badge or a medal pinned above her heart. She was not smiling nor frowning, her pale face and dark eyes peering into the camera matter of factly. Her eyes showed intelligence and sensitivity and her thin face and delicate hands accentuated the intelligent, sensitive eyes.

I studied the century old photograph for several minutes wishing the girl's eyes could explain how such a pretty and delicate young woman became a prostitute. There was no need for her to explain to me or anyone else, how she came to live the life she had; still, I was curious.

Two envelopes lay beside her photograph. One was addressed to Rosa May at 18 D Street, the other, at 32 South D Street, Virginia City, Nevada. I knew about Virginia City from watching the Bonanza television show. Virginia City was another mining town. I had no idea when the town flourished. Rosa May had apparently lived in Virginia City before coming to Bodie.

In the upper right hand corner of each envelope, there was an oval green stamp with the white, embossed figurehead of George Washington. In the upper, curved portion of the stamp above Washington, "U.S. Postage," was written, and below, "Three Cents." Over the stamp, a faded blue postmark was stamped, but I was unable to read where the letter was posted. Each letter had been carried by Wells, Fargo and Co. whose stages were robbed in the movies.

I admired the ornate Victorian script in which both letters were addressed. The letters curled and twisted ever so neatly. The lines were thin where the writers used little pressure; but where they had pressed hard, the quill had opened wider and more ink had flowed onto the paper, making a darker, thicker stroke.

Though Rosa's gravestone did not give her year of death, it occurred to me that a catalog of U.S. stamps could pinpoint the years the green, three cent, stamped envelopes were used. Knowing the years would give me some clue of when Rosa May had lived in Virginia City.

Some weeks later, I learned that the three cent envelope was manufactured by the Plimpton Manufacturing Company at Hartford, Connecticut, and was distributed from 1874 to 1886. Sometime during that twelve year span, Rosa May had lived in Virginia City.

The envelopes offered a clue to Rosa's character: she had neatly opened each envelope at the narrow, right edge with a sharp letter knife. The knife had cut so clean you had to look closely to see that the edge was slightly torn. One might deduce as an amateur Sherlock Holmes, that Rosa May was a woman of habit and she was neat.

Having wandered through the museum and the rest of the ghost town, fascinated by the old place, I drove back to Mammoth.

All songs begin in the unconscious mind, stimulated and pushed into the conscious mind by a triggering of emotions. Somewhere during my night's sleep, that triggering of emotions had taken place and I awoke, with a simple, folk-like melody in my head. I took quick advantage of my good fortune. I laid in bed and listened to the melody, to its rising and falling. When I was certain I had the tune memorized, I reached for my Martin D-28. The battered, old guitar had been with me for five years, and had helped me write more than 200 love songs.

The harmony chords for the tune were simple: four chords, G, A minor, C and D. The song had two basic parts: the melody of the verse and the melody of the chorus. There would be no bridge—no middle section; just verse, chorus, A and B.

I began singing the melody out loud accompanying it with a slight country rhythm. I sang "la, las" and "doo-dee-doos" for syllable sounds. I gradually replaced the syllable sounds with words—any words—searching for a word would sound best with each note. Round open mouth sounds like long "O's" as in Bo-die, fit best for lower notes. Long E's, as in EE-ZY, fit best on high notes when the throat constricts. I had gone through this word sorting process for more than twelve years and by now it was a mechanical, unconscious process.

The simple melody seemed to suit Bodie, with its brown,

weathered buildings, the sagebrush, its graveyard overrun with weed, its romance and legends. But it was the image of Rosa May's banished grave and pretty face that stood out in my mind. Somehow in the mystery of the creative process, the lyrics came to me within two hours. The rough draft went like this:

> Somewhere in northern California
> There's a ghost town the miners once called Bodie
> And on a hilltop just outside of Bodie
> There stands a stone that simply reads, "Rosa May"
>
> And all the miners who lived back in seventy-nine
> Told of her beauty in the saloons and in the mines
> Though the women sneered whenever she walked their
>   way
> All the miners smiled when they saw Rosa May
>
> **Chorus**
> Rosa May you know I never knew you
> But your story's like music to my ears
> How you comforted the poor, lonely miners
> Can bring a lonesome soul like me to tears
>
> Though the miners paid her for her love
> She was a woman they always spoke fondly of
> A fallen angel with a heart of gold they say
> that was the beautiful, the beautiful Rosa May
>
> **Chorus**
> Rosa May you know I never knew you
> But your story's like music to my ears
> How you comforted the poor, lonely miners
> Can bring a lonesome soul like me to tears
>
> Now today, as I walk these streets of Bodie
> The miners are gone and the gold has long been spent
> The streets are still and the wind whistles through the
>   grass

Buildings brown and burn beneath a hot summer sun
All that's left are the diggings and the mines
Forgotten dreams of thousands of lonely miners
And on a hilltop where the wind blows through the sage-
brush
There stands a stone that simply reads, "Rosa May"

Chorus

After I learned more about Rosa's story, I rewrote the lyrics. The last two verses on the recorded version are different and fit her story better.

After I finished the lyrics, I sang the song over and over. I was happy with the way it turned out. Some songs a writer feels closer to than others. "Rosa May" was that kind of song for me.

Rosa May's outcast grave struck a sensitive chord in me. Rosa May was a prostitute. She was different and was ostracized for her difference. She had lived on the outskirts of society. Finally, she was denied burial in the Bodie Cemetery. From the outset, that seemed terribly unfair.

Rosa May's story was something I could relate to. Like everyone, there were times I had felt like an outsider. A lot of that came from growing up in a troubled home.

I identified with Rosa May for another reason: Rosa May was a prostitute. Playing in bars I sometimes felt like I had sold out. I traded my creative talents for money, to pay bills, to eat. I often worked places where I did not belong. I often entertained people with whom I had little in common, and often, little respect. I did it for money.

It was a fact of life you learned to live with. But sometimes it led you to drink too much and fool yourself too much and do too many crazy things you shouldn't do to yourself or to those with whom you did them.

There was another reason I could identify with Rosa May as an outsider. I was an artist living in a society which respected money, power and success above all things. Successful artists, those who had learned to convert their art into a commercial product—they too were respected. It was the struggling artist between failure and success with whom society did not know how to deal. All artists go through times of paying their dues. If you are strong, gifted and lucky, those times strengthen you and helped you refine your craft. But if you grow weary of the struggle, and become disheartened, they can make you feel like giving up before you grab hold of the golden ring. It was something you should not think about late into the night and alone after too many drinks. For you knew self-pity was self-destructive.

So there were the moments of loneliness which had taken the unknown woman—Rosa May—and unconsciously made her a kind hearted comforter of Bodie's lonely miners. That was how the song worked for me. The thought of a kind hearted woman comforting lonely miners somehow comforted me.

Inspired by the Rosa May song, the next day I made another trip to Bodie and once more joggled over the Cottonwood Canyon road. Again I climbed the sage covered hill to Rosa Mays grave.

Rosa May's misshapen marker seemed to plead for pity. My God, how bad could she have been not to be forgiven in death?

At the Bodie Museum I approached the young woman hired by the State Parks Service there to answer visitors's questions about Bodie's history.

"Does you know anything about Rosa May," I asked, pointing to Rosa's display case.

"Over there," she nodded toward a book rack holding numerous books on Bodie history. "There's a book by Ella Cain. There's a story in her book about Rosa May." She smiled, "Many are curious about Rosa May." I didn't want to hear that. I wanted to believe that I was the only one interested in her life.

I picked up the yellow paperback, *The Story of Bodie*, by Ella Cain.

Born in 1882 in Bodie, Ella Cain grew up in the camp and later taught school there. Over the years she collected a stories she had heard told since childhood. One of these was the story of Rosa May.

Accompanying Cain's story, was a photograph of Rosa May, taken at the age of about twenty-four. In my song I had said Rosa May was beautiful. This photo showed exactly how beautiful she was. With her mouth closed, she smiled innocently at the camera, posing in a long sleeved, black velvet dress. I stared at her for several minutes admiring her beauty, feeling odd to have written a song about her.

Paraphrased, Cain's story goes something this:

Virgin Alley had a new sign, *The Highgrade,* over the latest house of ill repute on the long street inhabited by the demimonde of the camp. Its occupant was a dark eyed, curly headed, petite French girl. Before coming to Bodie she had lived at 18 South D Street, Virginia City and at No 1 Ormsby Street, Carson City.

After a very short time in Bodie, Rosa May became the toast and idol of the men who frequented the sporting district, and there were many. One miner said of her, "She was a gal who had a smile you'd go to hell for and never regret it." Rosa May was the undisputed queen of Bodie's underworld.

Ernest Marks, proprietor of the Laurel Palace Saloon, fell in love with Rosa and she with him. Marks wasn't bad looking, tall and dark with a slight mustache. True to his Hebrew blood, Marks had inherited the traditional trait of making money. He lavished plenty of it on Rosa in diamonds and furs.

One evening a Cornishman, Billy Owens, attempted to toast Rosa May in Marks' saloon. Marks, easily made jealous, pulled a gun from under the counter and threatened to use it if Billy or anyone else toasted Rosa. From that time on, there was bad blood between Marks and Owens.

Shortly afterwards, Rosa took a trip abroad and visited her native Paris. She flitted about Brussels and Berlin and came to a standstill in Monte Carlo. There she gambled away thousands of dollars miners had lost in Marks's saloon.

Rosa at last returned to Bodie bringing with her ten or fifteen trunks filled with finery and many jewels. She replaced the red lantern that hung on her porch with a fine hand wrought iron lantern with red panel glass. She also brought silver door knobs, fine furniture and mirrors and spread them throughout the house.

While Rosa was away, the Fortuna Ledge was discovered in the Standard Mine. Rosa came by a fair share of the highgrade miners snuck out of the mine.

With the highgrade ore, Rosa May bought more diamonds from Frank Golden, the jeweler. She had Frank make a pair of cuff links and matchbox from the highgrade. The frames were made of gold and faced with gold-quartz. On the back of the matchbox, E.M. was engraved and below the initials, the figure of a cupid. Rosa gave the matchbox and cuff links to Marks who often showed them off.

A hard, cold winter hit, deep snows, below zero temperatures, pneumonia weather. A pneumonia epidemic struck the camp. Rosa went from one miner's cabin to another nursing the stricken men. She penned many letters home for the dying men. But the time came when she could no longer go on her mission of mercy. Rosa may contracted pneumonia. In a few days she was dead.

They buried Rosa in the outcast cemetery. Marks had a picket fence placed around her grave. "Someday," he told himself, "Rosa will have a fitting monument," but the day never came although Rosa left him a fortune in cash and diamonds.

Bad luck hit Bodie. The rich Fortuna Ledge faulted and was lost. The boom camp became a ghost town. Only a few old timers held on, Ernest Marks and Billy Owens were two. Over the long years, they forgave one another. Occasionally, the old men played cards to pass the day.

Each day, Ernest's gambling hall and saloon were empty. He lost his fortune and one by one, sold Rosa's jewels far below their worth. Finally there was nothing left to sell but the matchbox and cuff links and a trunk of Rosa's finery and keepsakes that Ernest had treasured all these years.

To make matters worse, Marks fell into lingering illness. Billy Owens nursed his old friend. Ernest's relatives in New York were notified of his condition. They sent him money until he died.

Ernest's last request was to be buried beside Rosa. Billy Owens dug the grave.

In time, Billy Owens died broke. In order to pay for his funeral expenses, the Sheriff auctioned off Billy's lodging house and all its contents. A trunk was brought out and sold. It contained the finery, pictures and letters of Rosa May. Found among the belongings were Ernest's matchbox and gold cuff links, the only items worth anything. The matchbox and cuff links paid for Billy's funeral.

So, Rosa May had comforted dying miners after all, had caught pneumonia and died. Was the story really true or was it simply another romanticized tale of the West?

"I'd take it with a grain of salt," the girl in the Museum said.

I felt odd to have written a song about a woman I knew nothing about, and strangely the song had some truth in it. Was it a coincidence my ballad of the good hearted whore spun a similar tale to Ella Cain's story, or was there someone out there trying to tell me something, struggling through death and eternity to vindicate herself?

After reading Ella Cain's story, now with additional information, I rewrote the lyrics to "Rosa May."

Somewhere in northern California,
There's a ghost town the miners once called Bodie.
And on a hilltop just outside of Bodie,
There stands a stone that simply reads, "Rosa May."

And all the miners who lived back in seventy-nine,
Told of her beauty in the saloons and in the mines.
Though the women sneered whenever she walked their
      way,
All the miners smiled when they saw Rosa May.

Chorus
Rosa May you know I never knew you,
But your story's like music to my ears.
How you comforted the poor, lonely miners,
Can bring a lonesome soul like me to tears.

Though the miners paid her for her love,
She was a woman they always spoke fondly of.
A fallen angel with a heart of gold they say,
that was the beautiful, the beautiful Rosa May.

Chorus

The story's still told of a hundred years ago,
Pneumonia killing miners, Bodie buried deep in snow.
Rosa went from one house to another,
Nursing miners, writing letters home to mothers.

Pneumonia took the good and bad they say,
And in the end took the beautiful Rosa May.
They buried her on a hilltop where today,
There stands a stone that simply reads "Rosa May."

Chorus
Rosa May you know I never knew you
But your story's like music to my ears.
How you comforted the poor, lonely miners,
Can bring a lonesome soul like me to tears.

Chapter 5

Seek, and you will find.— Jesus

I studied the photo of the pretty young woman a considerable time each day, seeking a clue to her life's story. I searched her eyes, her innocent smile, the way she folded her arms, the shape of her eyebrows, the way she had brushed back her curly, brown hair showing her ear; noticed too, her dark velvet dress with three buttons at the elbow, the high collar tight around her neck—a fashion long outmoded.

Little Rosa's shoulders barely reached the back of a kitchen chair. I wondered what lived behind her happy eyes, what made her seem so content? Who had snapped this only photo of her, in what city, what year? Whoever he was, he had caught Rosa in the spring of her life with his miracle machine and this image was all that was left of her.

I carried this image of Rosa's pretty face on my return trips to Bodie as I walked through the sagebrush to her grave, and crept over the barren hills surrounding the cluster of rotting buildings that had been Rosa's last home. During these trips, and in the months to come, I always tried to imagine what Rosa's life had been like here in this mining camp.

My imagination soared. Here, in this small valley below, where tourists wandered with cameras dangling from their necks, entirely different sights and sounds lived when Rosa was alive. The valley and the nearby hills had been covered with flimsy buildings. Children ran through the streets as teams of horses brought in supplies. Bodie Bluff had been a beehive of activity. Men, horses and wagons went up and down the narrow roads; ore wagons filled with rich rock, crept down to the mills with their burdens, the ore gobbled by wooden shoots and pulverized by tons of steel. The stamp mills, yes—and the Standard Mill still standing at the foot of Bode Bluff, they had pounded day and night, their roaring had filled the valley, the white smoke had climbed upward out of the tall, black stacks into the blue sky. Men had struggled and prayed the rich Fortuna vein would hold out so prosperity might continue.

Men, rich and poor, had raced through the streets speaking excitedly of this new strike in this or that mine. The stage came and went, saloons roared day and night, men gambled at poker tables, men gambled with Bodie stocks, prostitutes gambled with their lives. And it was all gone, lost behind the veil of time, the life Rosa had lived, the sights and sounds she had taken for granted. Now here I was on a hilltop, reaching with my imagination, my questions, my theories. Could I ever really know what life was like here in Bodie?

In my mind, Rosa's eyes stared steadily into mine. Was it possible for any woman—even a prostitute— to be happy living in such a reckless and wild a place as Bodie, with whisky-mouthed men, pounding her door night and day, anxious to go down into the heat of her tiny body for as long as she would permit? Could this life make any woman happy or was this simply a means of living, something Rosa was doing in the meantime, until something better came along? Or was Rosa like other whores who fooled themselves, believing someday, some wonderful man would come along and sweep them away from the hell they lived? There were so many questions, so much I wanted to know and didn't.

I walked alone through a large open field at the far north end of Bodie. Cattle grazed here, and blackbirds twittered in the grass. Few tourists wandered this field as I. They did not know that it was here in Chinatown where the Bodie red light district once stood. The Chinese had lived on King Street, which ran off Main Street. Here they built their joss houses and opium dens, and from here carted their vegetables uptown.

Bonanza Street, or Virgin Alley as it was most often called, sprouted north from King Street and ran the length of the field just behind and parallel to Main Street. Back doors of the Main Street saloons emptied the miners directly into the red light district. Here along Bonanza Street, the row of cribs stood, small frame shacks where the prostitutes lived and worked. The cribs and their women, the Chinese and the saloons, were all gone. Part of Chinatown burned down in the 1932 fire that wiped out seventy percent of Bodie. The remaining buildings were later torn down. Chinatown's inhabitants had left behind their heaps of trash, rusting tins, busted bottles violet with age, square holes now eaten up by summer grass where outhouses once stood. You could just barely see a slight indentation running through the field where Bonanza Street once was. It had been many years since that road carried a man "down the line."

My mind wandered on. In summer, those girls who were not busy with customers, would have come out of their cribs in the late afternoon to sit on the stoops, casting their sleepy eyes toward Bodie Bluff, watching the thick-backed men, very aware that their coming and going put the bread in their bellies and the gold in their purses. There would be name calling and threats and laughter among the women. One or two would already be drunk. Others would defiantly wait for the shriek of the shift whistle.

Some of the women were young and pretty like Rosa May; some were old and beaten. Many were unhappy and reckless, a matter of time before they did themselves in. Yet each woman knew this: Bodie was a mining camp with many men and few women. Money could be made from man's need for woman. These women were whores but were needed here as much as the men who worked the hot depths of Bodie Bluff.

But of all the women who had lived and worked in this field I now walked, only one was still remembered, one honored, one spoken of among tourists and neighboring residents. It was Rosa May. And why? Because a legend had grown up around her name, a story of a kind hearted whore who died while nursing miners. Word of mouth, generation after generation, had made Rosa a saint. Ella Cain had furthered the legend with her account of Rosa May. All who had spoken well of Rosa expressed their child-like faith in the inherent goodness of legends, of vague people who lived long ago and did wonderful things. Who could think badly of Rosa May now, even if she was a whore? She had died a martyr legend claimed. Now romance surrounded her name and people wanted to believe their romantic notions. For Rosa's story flavored Bodie's bygone days with sentiment.

As I sang "Rosa May" in the Whisky Creek bar, weekenders tuned in and paid attention. Without fail, someone would come up during breaks, with eager eyes, hungry to know more about Rosa May, a "lady of the evening." I was made aware that I was not alone in my curiosity.

The idea of a book about Rosa's life began to bob in the back of my mind. To write such a book would require a great deal of research. It would also take a lot of time and money. I could make the time, but money would be a problem.

There was another problem. I had never done historical research. How and where was one to begin?

One could start with people. Locate old-timers who had lived in Bodie and possibly known Rosa May or something about her.

At this time, I believed Rosa May died around 1880 as her marker vaguely claimed. The chance of finding anyone alive who might have known Rosa was slim. Still, there was a chance.

Second, there were books. I had read Ella Cain's *The Story of Bodie*, and noticed several other books about Bodie in the Bodie Museum. Through these I might discover more about Rosa May.

Third, old newspapers of the era might also provide information. If Rosa May had been well known, my chances of finding items on her were good. If she was not well known, research would be more difficult. Certainly something about her would show up if I searched hard and long enough.

And fourth, public records might provide facts about her life. Bodie being within Mono County, records for Bodie would most likely be found at Bridgeport, Mono County seat.

It was now mid-July. Kevin and I would be at Whisky Creek until August 1. Following this, we had a week engagement near Lake Tahoe. I had about three weeks in the area to research before heading south to record our album.

In her story, Ella Cain provided some information on Rosa May. I planned to investigate this information. Most of this could be done at the Bridgeport courthouse where death and land records are kept. I hoped something would turn up regarding Rosa May, Ernest Marks and Billy Owens.

As Highway 395 winds down from Conway Summit, you enter a wide green valley an hour north of Mammoth. Just outside town you pass cattle grazing in the moist fields and water in ditches beside the road. Red-winged blackbirds dangle from barbed wire fences. The air smells warm and earthy from the water and the moist fields. This would be a nice place to live. The wide valley feels calm.

The little settlement of Bridgeport rests quietly beside the East Walker River, with the dark Sierra, some peaks still patched with snow, to the west. The town is no more than a couple blocks long, with several restaurants, sporting good stores and motels. If you blink, you might pass Bridgeport, head into the mountains and north to Carson City. The pioneer settlement of Bridgeport has managed to survive while the nearby boom camps of Bodie, Masonic and Lucky Boy have come and gone.

The most conspicuous building in Bridgeport is the two story wooden courthouse, snow white and trimmed in bright red, built in 1880, the second year of Bodie's boom. The Bridgeport people take excellent care of the old courthouse and do not permit pigeons to roost in the high nooks below the roof. Chicken wire protects these places from their would-be messy inhabitants.

My first objective was to discover when Rosa May died. Knowing her time of death, I could limit research to the preceding years. Time of death would also help determine how feasible it was to locate people who knew Rosa May.

I was excited as I walked to the county clerk's office down the halls of high ceilings and rich hard woods. I explained to an elderly, gray haired lady what I was doing. She kindly led me to a huge vault, its thick steel door stood open. Inside the vault were stacks of old leather bound volumes, you could smell their years inside the musty vault.

The clerk explained that the deceased would be listed in an index. There were several indexes, each covering a period of years. I was limiting my search at this point, between 1865-1900. I thought this to be a fair span. Once I found a name I was looking for, beside the name would be a volume and a page number which would contain the actual death certificate.

When searching for ownership of land, there were similar indexes. These were called Grantor-Grantee indexes; the grantor, being the seller; the grantee, the buyer.

The clerk left the vault and I opened the index of deaths to the "M" section for "May." As I ran my finger down the long column of names, struggling to read the ornate Victorian script, I discovered that the names were not in alphabetical order. What should have been a simple task had now become an ordeal of going down column after column, page after page of names.

I spent that morning searching the indexes of death and land records. I did not find a single reference to Rosa May. As far as Mono County records went, Rosa May had not owned land nor had she died in Bodie. Perhaps a negligent physician had failed to notify authorities of Rosa's death, or perhaps authorities hadn't cared to list the death of a prostitute. Then again, I had recently learned of two disastrous fires in Bodie, in 1892 and 1932. Perhaps a death record at Bodie was destroyed in one of the fires. However, county clerks assured me, all of Bodie's public records were always kept at Bridgeport. If Rosa May died in Bodie, county records should bear proof. But they didn't.

I left the courthouse and walked to a nearby hamburger stand. I refueled with a barbecue beef and a large root beer. If county records showed nothing, how would I learn anything substantial about her life?

Fortunately, Ella Cain mentioned in her story the names of Ernest Marks, Rosa's lover, and Billy Owens. After lunch I went back to the courthouse vault.

That afternoon, I managed to gather the first information about Rosa May, Ernest Marks and Billy Owens.

The first record I found on Ernest Marks was a land transaction. He had sold lot 52 of block 21 in Bodie to Charles Kuhlman for twenty dollars June 13, 1898. I was surprised to find the year 1898. I had figured that Rosa, Ernest and Billy had died before this time. Not so. In fact, Ernest Marks' death certificate states he died July 28, 1928, from heart failure and chronic prostatitis.

Born in Prussia in 1853, Marks was seventy-five at death. His death certificate made it clear, that Billy Owens, the undertaker, buried Ernest in the Odd Fellows Cemetery. Here was the first discrepancy between Ella Cain's account and county records. The Odd Fellows Cemetery was located inside the regular Bodie cemetery. If Billy had buried Ernest inside the fence, then Ernest was not buried beside Rosa in the outcast cemetery as Ella Cain claimed.

Also, while last in Bodie, I had made a point of checking this out and found that there was no evidence of another grave beside Rosa's—no marker, no mound of dirt, no grave. I was inclined to believe that Rosa was buried in the outcast cemetery by herself, and that Ella Cain had simply let her imagination run to give her story a sentimental ending. I was beginning to question Cain's information.

Billy Owens' death certificate states he was born April 7,1855 in Missouri. He died September 4, 1933 in Bodie from a heart attack. Billy had lived in the Bodie area for fifty years. He worked in the mines, became an undertaker and later, Justice of the Peace. His mother was A.J. Johnson.

Land records revealed that Billy had owned lots 23 and 24 of block 11 in Bodie. This property, the buildings, and all within were sold at a Sheriffs auction July 25, 1934, to pay for Billy's funeral just as Ella Cain said in her story. A certain B.C. Honea had purchased Billy's property for $50.

At the mention of Billy's property, I remembered Ella Cain told of a certain trunk that had belonged to Rosa which was sold after Rosa's death. Her trunk, which contained clothing, photos and letters, came into Ernest's keeping and later fell into Billy's hands when Ernest died. If I found B.C. Honea, whoever he was and if he was still alive, I might find the letters that had once belonged to Rosa May. Such letters could provide first hand information about her life. They were invaluable. I would have to locate B.C. Honea. He might still live still in the area.

For now, I was through with county records. I walked out of the musty vault into the bright July sun. My eyes were sore, my head throbbed. A little tired but I was still energized. I must somehow find a lead on someone who could provide specific information about Rosa May. I was happy to have learned something about Ernest Marks and Billy Owens. That they had died as late as 1928 and 1933 was encouraging. I might after all find someone still alive who had known Rosa May.

My next thought was the Mono County Museum. Perhaps the museum might have books or information about Rosa

40

May. The curator might also provide leads on old-timers who had lived in Bodie.

I walked over to the museum and quickly went through its numerous exhibits seeking two words: Rosa May. I found a colored print of a middle-aged woman in a dress that looked as if it might have been worn in the 1890's. The type written note below it said the print was Rosa May, a Bodie "hurdy-gurdy girl of the 1880's and 90's." I doubted the print was of Rosa May. It looked nothing like her photo, but I wanted to know who at the museum knew about Rosa living in Bodie in the 1890's.

At the entrance, I found a thin, middle aged man, bent over a large canvas. He was painting a Western scene of a prairie schooner and sagebrush in water colors. He hardly noticed me staring at him while he worked. He dipped his brush into the colors, made a tiny stroke on the canvas, dipped the brush in clean water, then back into the colors again. I thought I should not disturb him, then remembered what little time was left before I had to go back to Southern California.

I introduced myself and told the painter what I was looking for. Keeping a keen eye on his work, he said he was the museum curator. I could see he didn't want to be bothered, but I figured he could help me if I kept at him.

I asked the curator about Ella Cain's story. He had known Ella; she was dead now. I was sorry. I had a lot of questions for her.

I said Ella didn't include dates in her story. Ella wasn't particular about dates, he said. I wondered if she was particular about other details. As far as he knew, Ella's Rosa May story was true.

And the print of Rosa May in the museum, where had that come from?

Someone had donated it, he didn't know who.

Who said Rosa was a hurdy-gurdy girl in the 1890's? He didn't know.

I asked about his painting, how long he had been at it, whether or not it had made him money.

At my interest in his work, the painter perked up. He had been painting a long while and his paintings had earned

41

large sums. Some of his paintings were in various museums.

I wasn't the first one to search for information regarding Rosa May. I was stung with jealously. I thought I was the only one who cared about her life. Not so. Many had searched for information. I wouldn't find anything, he warned; no one had. But for what it was worth, there was an old man, Bill Glenn, who used to work around the museum who had always spoken well of Rosa May. Glenn was born in Bodie and now lived in Oakland. Perhaps he could help me. The curator gave me Glenn's address and I thanked him.

I drove back to Mammoth, content to have found something. I would write Bill Glenn to learn what he knew about Rosa May.

In the following weeks, I read several books about Bodie. Though informative as to Bodie's history and mining camp life, they only mentioned Rosa May in passing.

End of July came and our gig at Whisky Creek was over. It had been a good gig. We had made some new friends, and the audiences had made the job a pleasure. We would miss Mammoth and the mountains.

We filled our cars with amplifiers and guitars and headed up Highway 395 toward Tahoe. At our next club we were given a cabin and meals, and our regular pay. The nights came and went; we met new faces but we would be gone soon. The lonesomeness of life without roots nagged us.

In this final week in the area, I made another trip to Bridgeport. You may remember that Rosa's marker was made by a man called Serventi. He wrote his name at the base of the marker. I believed Serventi knew Rosa May and may have been a neighbor. I planned to check this out by going through land records.

In the Bridgeport courthouse, I found a deed dated October 6, 1890, which stated that a certain Antonio Serventi, sold lots 26 and 30 of block 26. Block 26 was the red light district; lots 2 and 30 were about a hundred feet behind Virgin Alley. Antonio Serventi could have been a Rosa's neighbor. Had Antonio made her marker?

In the phone book I found a Louis Serventi in Bishop

south of Mammoth Lakes. Hoping there was a chance Louis was related to Antonio Serventi, I called him. An aged, raspy voice answered the phone. It was Louis Serventi and he spoke with a thick Italian accent.

"Mr. Serventi?"

"Yesa."

"My name is George Williams. I'm doing research on Rosa May of Bodie. Was Antonio Serventi a relative of yours?"

"He was my uncle. He dead a long time. Die in the twenties." I couldn't believe my luck.

"He lived in Bodie in the 1890's?"

"Yesa. He come to America from the old country. Then go to the gold strikes in Colorado, then come to Bodie. I remember him telling us children stories about Bodie."

"Did he ever mention Rosa May?"

"Ah ... No, he never menshun Rosie May."

"Her gravestone has Serventi written on it. I think Antonio might have made it for her."

"No, Uncle Antonio not make Rosies marker. I make it."

"You made it!"

"Yesa. I make it long time ago."

"When?"

"Les see... I still had the Jeep. Maybe 1965 or so."

"Why did you make it for her? Did you know Rosa May?"

"No, I not know Rosie May. She a good woman. I read about her in the book"

"What book?"

"Uh..."

"You scribbled 1880 on her marker. How do you know she died in 1880?"

"The book say so."

"The Ella Cain book?"

"Yesa, I think so."

There were no dates in Ella's story.

"Look Mr. Serventi, this is long distance. I can't keep it any longer. I'll write you a letter. You've been very helpful."

I hung up and copied his address out of the phone book. When I finally visited Louis Serventi in Bishop, I found him a very kind man of 83, his deep brown nose drooping over his lip. He had been wrong about Rosa's year of death. His error opened the possibility that Rosa May might have died years later. Perhaps, I hoped, someone was still alive who had known her.

Louis Serventi lived in a large house surrounded by flowers with a daughter who had been mentally crippled by spinal meningitis. I couldn't believe it when he introduced us.

"This is Rosa," he said.

We drove back down Highway 395, past Bridgeport, Mammoth and Bishop. We crossed the hot Mojave Desert at night, the warm August air in through the windows, we smelled the dryness of the desert. As we neared San Bernardino, we smelled the smog. We'd been away from smog for two months breathing clean Sierra air. Now the odor was sickening.

We left the high Mojave Desert and weaved down the Cajon Pass into San Bernardino. The smog grew thicker the closer we got to San Bernardino, one of the most severely polluted cities in the world.

A friend had recently married and I was to watch his house while he honeymooned. This worked out well. I planned to move nearer to Hollywood as soon as possible; I didn't want the hassle of looking for a temporary apartment.

While house-sitting, I began to write a novel about Rosa May. I had to use my imagination because I knew very little about her. After working out a first chapter, it was clear I needed to know about Rosa's life to write a novel.

Fortunately, our record producer was working on another project that would keep him busy until September. This gave me some time to go back to the Bodie area for more research.

Before leaving for Bridgeport, I wrote Bill Glenn in Oakland and Louis Serventi in Bishop. Bill Glenn was quick to reply. Born in 1899, Bill Glenn was seventy-seven. He remembered Rosa May, Ernest Marks and Billy Owens from his childhood. He recalled Rosa May handing out dimes to children in the street. He could not remember what she looked like. He remembered Ernest Marks as a small man who was lame and had the gout. Billy Owens was "just a regular guy" who did odd jobs and later became Bodie's undertaker.

Of the three, Rosa died first, he didn't know when. Marks, he claimed, was buried beside her. He thought much of what he remembered might have been things he overheard his parents say. He believed Ella's story about Rosa dying while helping miners. At that time in Bodie, there was great fear of epidemics: pneumonia, scarlet fever and diphtheria as these diseases took many lives.

In reply to a question about a town paper, Bill said the *Bodie Miner*, published papers up until 1908-09. Jim Nugent, publisher and editor, took over the *Bridgeport Chronicle-Union* when the *Bodie Miner* folded.

This was about all Bill Glenn knew. He urged me to talk with Stuart and Sadie Cain in Bridgeport, who would know more.

Louis Serventi's reply explained more specifically, that Antonio came to America in his early twenties, headed for the Colorado gold strikes and later came to Bodie, where he worked at the Mono Mills, a lumber outfit about thirty miles south of Bodie, on the southeastern shore of Mono Lake.

Louis Serventi had known an old man who was a friend of Rosa May's and Ernest Marks. The old man said that Ernest was in fact buried beside Rosa. Before he died, he asked Louis to make Rosa May a marker. As luck would have it, the man was now dead.

As a child of eight or nine, Bill Glenn would have seen Rosa around 1908. With Billy Owens and Ernest Marks dying as late as 1928 and 1933, there was a chance someone who knew Rosa May might still be alive.

In the night, I loaded my VW bug with sleeping bag, Coleman stove, lantern, fuel and a cooler full of food and drink. I headed up the Cajon pass and across the Mojave Desert, back to Bodie, hoping to find the man or woman who long ago was Rosa May's friend.

Chapter 6

As I sped down the dark two lane desert highway toward Bishop, I had plenty of time to consider what I was doing. Strange how suddenly my thoughts were taken up with a mining camp prostitute.

A month before, I couldn't have imagined driving hundreds of miles seeking the story of a life lived years before I was born. And yet, here I was, in the middle of the desert, obsessed enough to spend my last two hundred dollars in the hopes of finding answers. I had no idea what I would do when the money was gone or where I'd live when I returned to Riverside. Somehow, things would work out.

Like every American kid, I was raised on TV westerns. All I knew about the wild West is what I'd seen on television. So I knew very little. Nor did I know much about mining camps or mining camp prostitutes except what I'd recently read. So it was easy for me to have romantic notions about the West and Rosa May's life. Her story in itself was romantic enough, blurred by enough years to make it seem a fairy tale. Buried in those distant years and in Rosa's vague story, was a real woman who had lived a life, very different from mine. I wanted to learn about that life for it had been lived in a romantic and fascinating era that I could never live in despite modern technology.

So there I was, a modern Don Quixote, speeding across the warm Mojave Desert in a VW bug, the warm alkaline air blowing my long hair back, trying my best to ride into Rosa May's past life. Over desert and mountain I was coming to Rosa's defense, hoping to unearth her life from years of misquoted stories and distorted facts. With my sword-like pen, I would tell her true story, the story I now imagined of a woman whose life had gone sadly astray. For at this time, Rosa May was no ordinary whore to me. Her martyr death had redeemed an otherwise ugly life, and its compassionate end, made her life as a whore more palatable to me and the thousands of grandmas who visit Bodie each year.

I promised myself I would do whatever I could to discover the truth. If her life in reality was the legend Ella Cain told of, I would be content. Like many of Rosa's believers, I too wanted to think the best of her. There was, of course, the possibility research might prove Cain's tale was a mere fabrication, that Rosa May had simply been a plain mining camp whore. I was tampering with a legend, one many wanted to believe. They wouldn't think kindly if I proved the legend they had taken to heart was a lie.

I laid my thoughts aside. I was getting tired. I switched on the radio to keep awake. I found a country music station. Country music and dark desert highways fit well.

In the early morning hours I had crossed most of the Mojave Desert and was now driving beneath the Sierra. I smelled the fresh water in the air and the damp, clean smell of wet sagebrush. The highway gleamed from a brief desert shower. I wanted to make Bishop, but I would settle for Independence, 42 miles south. I was bone tired when I reached Independence. I pulled off at a rest area and drove down a dirt road lined with trucks and campers. I parked far from the noise of the highway. I laid a ground cloth on the dirt and crawled into my sleeping bag. I went right to sleep. In less than four hours the sun would be blazing.

By 6:30 the desert sun was roaring down on my nylon sleeping bag making it impossible to sleep any longer. I wrapped up the bag, threw it in the car and with tired eyes drove to Bishop.

In Bishop I grabbed a quick breakfast and drove over to Louis Serventi's. I wanted to interview him again and jog his memory on a few details.

It had been many years since Louis' friend died, the old man who had known Ernest Marks and Rosa. Louis tried hard to remember his name. It might have been Mike or John, he wasn't certain. It was too long ago for him to recall. Louis offered me the addresses of his cousins, Margherita and Louise, the daughters of Antonio Serventi.

Louise and Margherita, ladies in their seventies, talked for an hour and a half about their father, Antonio. They brought out an old photo album of Antonio's, the red velvet cover now worn with handling, the figure of an antlered buck embossed on the cover. We three went through the old photos together, me hoping to find another photo of Rosa May. Unlikely, but worth a try.

Antonio was a warm, charitable man, a laborer with a fine gift for storytelling. Louise and Margherita had listened many hours to Antonio's tales of Bodie and other mining camps.

Born in 1852, he sailed from Italy to New York in his early twenties, made his way to Colorado searching for gold, then came to California. The old ladies could not recall Antonio telling them when he lived in Bodie. They thought it was after the boom years. They were surprised when I told them Antonio had owned land behind the Bodie red light district in the 1890's. He had never mentioned owning land in Bodie.

They told me Antonio had worked at the Mono Mills and later made charcoal for use in the Bodie mines. He left Bodie when Tonopah, Nevada boomed in the early 1900's. He later moved to Big Pine where he met his wife, Marie. He was forty-eight when he married. Eventually, Antonio and Marie moved to Bishop where Antonio built their home and farmed on six acres.

Unfortunately, but to be expected, they could not remember Antonio ever speaking of Rosa May. I believed he may have known Rosa May, perhaps had even spent a few dollars on her. With Antonio dying in 1920, many answers went with him. I thought it an irony how Louis Serventi, seventy years later, had made Antonio's neighbor, Rosa May, a grave marker.

For now, I was finished in Bishop. I was eager to climb out of the hot Owens Valley into the cool mountains, then on to Bodie.

As I drove up the steep incline to the mountains, my engine began giving me trouble. I had had the engine rebuilt two months earlier. I was warned it might last a month or a year. I angrily figured the engine wasn't going to last, and I had little money on me to fix it if it broke down. I was concerned but I would go on. I prayed the car would hold together until I got back to Riverside.

It was good to be in the mountains again. With my mind

busy figuring out ways to learn more about Rosa's life, the two and a half hour drive to Bodie seemed to fly. I passed Mammoth and Lee Vining and circled Mono Lake. Years ago, the Mono Mills had sawn timber on the lake's southeastern shore. It was there Antonio worked.

From 1881 to 1917 a light guage railroad ran from Mono Mills around the eastern shore and north and up the mountains to Bodie. The train twisted up steep switchbacks and arrived on top of Bodie Bluff. It was not a passenger train; it was only used to carry huge amounts of wood to fire the stamp mill and warm the miners' cottages. Chinese woodcutters also gathered wood in the nearby hills and hauled it to Bodie on squads of burros. They sold the wood to the mills and to the townspeople who were always afraid of a wood famine. If there was no wood, the mills could not operate and the men could not work.

In Bodie I walked the haunted streets and the field where Rosa had lived and died, then up the hill to her grave. There I paused a moment, wishing she might speak or a major relevation might come. None came. I walked back down the hill, passing tourists, remembering how a month earlier I had first visited Bodie.

In the Bodie Museum I reexamined Rosa's photograph, her clothing, and the envelopes addressed to her. The envelopes caught my attention. Perhaps there were return addresses and names on the backs of the envelopes. Names and addresses could certainly help me. I asked the girl who watched over the museum if she would turn the envelopes over. She looked at me strangely and said, no. Disappointed, I left the museum.

On Main Street I noticed a middle-aged blond woman dressed in a long Victorian dress, her hair neatly pinned up in the 1890's fashion. She was Ardie Adkisson, wife of Bob Adkisson, head park ranger. I introduced myself and told her what I was doing. Ardie Adkisson was a Rosa May enthusiast; we got along.

My first leads to old-timers came from Ardie who had met several on their occasional visits to Bodie to reminisce. From one elderly gentleman, Ardie heard that Rosa had fallen in love with a gambler, a real low-life. Another old-timer said Rosa May had been a madam in five mining camps: Virginia City, Bodie, Masonic, Lundy and Columbia.

In the local area there were several old-timers who might be able to help me. Ardie gave me their names and addresses.

In Bishop, there was Richie Conway, who had lived in Bodie as a kid and knew a lot about Bodie's early days. In Smith Valley, there was a Mrs. Bell, in her nineties, who had lived in Bodie for years. Her son, Bob Bell, was out in Luning, Nevada. Bob Bell knew a lot about Bodie's early days but he was shy.

Ardie had also met the niece of an old chinaman, who in earlier days, drove stage between Bodie and Hawthorne, Nevada. Ardie gave me the niece's address.

In Mono City, there was Frank Balfe who seemed to know a great deal about Rosa May. Ardie gave me directions.

I explained to Ardie about the return addresses on Rosa's envelopes. She too was curious. We went back into the museum and Ardie opened the locked display case. Turning the envelopes over, there were no names or addresses. We were disappointed.

As I drove to nearby Mono City to interview Frank Balfe, I wondered if Rosa May really was a madam at five mining camps, or whether she had fallen in love with a gambler as Ardie heard. I would hear lots of stories. I would have to carefully sift them to find the truth.

In Mono City, I found Frank Balfe's house with no trouble; Ardie gave me good directions. In the last ten years, Frank Balfe had taken a genuine interest in the Rosa May legend and had managed to gather some good information. Most of this came from Father Birks, an old man who served as a watchman at Bodie for several years. Father Birks was supposedly a priest and Bodie was one of his first parishes. Frank had met Birks in the late 1950's on a trip to Bodie. Birks was dead now, buried in the Bodie cemetery.

Father Birks remembered Rosa May as an older woman, about 57 or 60. I was surprised to hear this. I had imagined Rosa dying young, still quite pretty. Not so, according to Birks. She had come from some place back east. Birks thought it was upstate New York. She had worked five or seven years in brothels in Carson and Virginia City. She had spent the majority of time in Carson City though she made trips to Bodie where she also lived.

In Bodie, she married a rich miner in later years. Birks could not remember the man's name. Thought it was a short Anglo-Saxon name with five or six letters. Having known Rosa well himself, Birks said she was indeed a good hearted woman, something many said of her. Birks recalled old man Scanivino. The Scanivinos lived for years at the Goat Ranch, nine miles south of Bodie on Cottonwood Canyon road. Old man Scanivino had known Rosa May. He had nothing but good to say about her. Scanivino, too, was buried in the Bodie cemetery.

Father Birks believed Rosa died in Carson City. As she had requested, her body was brought back to Bodie for burial. I wondered if this was the reason I was unable to find a record of death in Mono County records. The townspeople would not allow Rosa to be buried in the regular cemetery. Nor would they allow her grave to be marked. Surprisingly, they did allow her husband burial inside the fence. This was all Birks knew about Rosa May.

Frank Balfe had one last bit of information. Several years ago while visiting the Bodie Museum, he saw a letter that Rosa May had written. It was in one of the display cases. Frank could not recall to whom the letter was written but it was clear that Rosa had written from Carson City to someone in Bodie. In her letter she wrote she had not been feeling well, that she had a cold or the chills. Frank could not remember the date the letter was written, but he stressed that it was from Carson City.

When Frank last visited Bodie, he was disturbed to discover the letter was missing from the glass display case. Elaine Bell, Bob Bell's wife, was curator of the museum at the time. I should ask Elaine about the letter. Frank stressed that the letter did exist.

I drove back to Bodie and searched the cemetery for Birks's grave. I found it. The marker read: Father Clarence C. Birks, 1897-1961, "Watchman" 1958-61. Because of his late birth, I doubted Birks knew Rosa May. If Bodie was one of his first parishes, it could not have been one until the 1920's. I later learned

51

that the Catholic church pulled out of Bodie by 1909. My suspicions about Birks were confirmed the next day by Bob Bell in Luning, Nevada.

From Bodie I drove sixty miles out into the Nevada desert to Hawthorne. It was evening when I arrived. Too tired for another interview, I hung around a casino watching those more confident in their luck lose their wallets over the green felt tables. Bored and tired, I headed towards Luning, twenty-five miles east of Hawthorne. I pulled off somewhere between Hawthorne and Luning, spread my sleeping gear on the dirt and spent a restless night listening to the lullabies of diesel trucks as they roared and rumbled down the highway into miles and more miles of desert.

The hot desert sun woke me early and I drove the remaining miles to Luning, nothing more than a gas station, a bar and a cluster of houses. At a roadside rest area I fixed some eggs and bacon and at 9 sharp I knocked on the door of Bob and Elaine Bell's mobile home

Fortunately, the Bell's were early risers. The door opened and Elaine Bell, a tall, outgoing, middle aged woman met me. I told her who I was and what I was doing. She asked me in where I met Bob Bell. Bob was about the same age, dressed in mechanics overalls, with wonderful impish eyes. He was, as Ardie said, a little shy but he seemed glad to answer my questions about Bodie.

Bob was born and raised in Bodie and was familiar with some of the town's stories. Unfortunately, he was born years after Rosa May's death but he did know something about her. He figured Rosa May came to Bodie in the camp's later years, perhaps the 1890's. He remembered Ernest Marks being crippled with rheumatism. Marks kept his saloon open until he died but he ended up broke.

Bob laughed when I mentioned Billy Owens. Owens was a funny little old man who was into everyone's business. Billy's mother, Grandma Johnson, ran a boarding house. Billy inherited the place when his mother died. Bob couldn't recall hearing the story about Rosa May dying while nursing miners. Nor could he recall hearing about the feud between Billy Owens and Ernest

Marks over Rosa.

Besides Rosa, there was another prostitute in Bodie, Emma Goldsmith. Emma, like Rosa, was a madam, but of the two houses, it seemed Emma's was more popular.

Bob figured Rosa May must have died in the 1890's. I asked Elaine Bell about the missing Rosa May letter. Elaine said there was no such a letter. She also said that the clothing in the museum which is supposed to be Rosa May's, was in fact Dolly Cain's, Jim Cain's daughter.

And about Father Birks, my suspicions were quickly confirmed. Bob Bell knew Birks personally and said, "Birks was no more a priest than you or I." Birks was married and before coming to Bodie he and his wife had lived in Bishop. If Birks had lied about being a priest, he could have lied about what he told Frank Balfe. However, I later learned that much of what Birks told Frank Balfe was true.

I believe much of Birks' information came from Ella Cain. It was the Cain family who had hired Birks as a Bodie watchman. During the three years he was watchman, Ella Cain was setting up the Bodie Museum. Ella and Birks had obviously talked about Rosa May. It was during these talks that Ella Cain passed on information only she knew. For it was Ella, I would later learn, who had found the Rosa May letters when Billy Owens' property was auctioned off. B.C. Honea had bought Billy's property. Ella had bought Rosa's trunk, full of clothing, photographs and personal letters. Ella had read the letters, some twenty-six, and learned the truth of Rosa's life. Some of this she told Birks, who with his wild imagination, distorted the facts here and there and finally imagined himself a personal acquaintance of Rosa's.

But I did not know any of this when I left Bob and Elaine Bell and drove across the desert back to Bishop. My mind whirled with all I had recently heard about Rosa's life. I didn't know what to believe.

It was then that I began to feel a strange presence in the car. I felt as if something or someone was pointing the way, opening doors, and would lead me to the truth. Something peculiar was happening, I felt it but I could not make sense of it, yet it was there near me. Something was about to turn up, something definite about Rosa's life.

And then my car began falling apart. At fifty it backfired and lost power. I figured the heads were loosening. Two months ago I had paid two hundred and fifty dollars to have the engine rebuilt and now this. I was not happy. I pulled over and lifted the hood up. I spit on the engine. The spit sizzled. The engine was overheating and if I wasn't careful it would blow up and I'd be stuck in the Nevada desert.

I let the engine cool down, hopped in and drove eighty miles to Bishop. In Bishop I found Richie Conway's house on the north edge of town. His farmhouse door was wide open but he was gone and stayed gone as long as I waited.

It was now about six in the evening and Bishop was still very hot. After driving all day, asking strangers questions and the car giving me trouble, I was frazzled. My money would last only so long. I couldn't keep this trip more than seven days and I was already into the third, and I wanted to learn so much more. And now Richie Conway wasn't home.

I drove down East Line Street and just before the bridge I turned right onto a dirt road and drove a half mile along the Owens River. I remembered a place I'd been to before, an open spot beside the river, nice and grassy. Here the Owens River was only twenty feet across.

I undressed and slid into the river. The freezing water, fresh out of the Sierra, sent shocks up my body. I found a shallow spot, bathed and got out. It was early evening but the sun was still hot. A hot breeze quickly dried my body. I shaved, using the car's outside mirror.

I pulled the Coleman stove out of the trunk, pumped the tank and lit the burner. I emptied a can of beans into a saucepan, cut up hot dogs and dropped them in. Seven minutes, dinner was ready. I dished the meal out, poured some cold milk, sat down and leaned against the fender.

I listened to the green water as it gurgled and calmly pushed against the river banks. Birds sang to their lovers in the bushes along the River. The smell of fresh water and cool, greenery swelled within me. The river pushed against the banks. A

54

tight feeling came into my throat. Exhaustion swept over me. My life at that moment seemed like an ocean without shores. The river I listened to at least had banks to push against. I too longed for someone to lean against. A man hates to admit it, but he needs boundaries. Without them, without someone to lean against in the night, there is no ease from the lonely dog barks in the back of your brain.

I rested after dinner, then drove back to Richie Conway's. He was still gone. I didn't want to hang around Bishop or sit in a bar all night. There was nothing in Bishop for me now. I drove ninety-four miles back to Bridgeport. There was plenty to do there tomorrow.

Chapter 7

I spent the night in Bridgeport camped beside the road, occasionally waking to the roar of diesels and the whisking of summer vacationers as their motors rushed, then faded into the distance. Up early, grabbed some milk and donuts at a market, and as soon as the courthouse opened, I was back in the vault, going over Mono County records, thinking I might have overlooked Rosa May the first time through. I also searched for records regarding Emma Goldsmith, supposedly the other Bodie madam. I did not find a single reference for either woman.

I was about to drive to Carson City when I thought of early Bodie newspapers. Asking around the courthouse, I was told that Slick Bryant, who ran the motel across the way, had a collection of Bodie newspapers.

The Bryants were one of the earliest pioneer families to settle in Bridgeport. In 1863, Amasa Foster Bryant was drawn to the region by the Aurora boom, a mining camp seventeen miles north of Bodie. Finding Aurora congested with businesses, he settled in Bridgeport and opened a general store. In 1877 he succumbed to Bodie's golden beckon and opened a store there, but returned to Bridgeport in 1881 when Bodie's mines declined.

His son, Amasa S. Bryant, also did his share of history making. A man of faith and vision, he believed in the telephone and brought its service to Bridgeport. His small telephone company ran lines out to Bodie and north to Fales Hot Spring.

Slick Bryant, son of Amasa S., was born in 1899, and but for a brief period, had lived his entire life in Bridgeport. Since the area was so sparsely settled, Slick knew most everybody. Slick would help me find families who had lived in Bodie.

Because of Slick's interest in preserving the local history, he was a big help often introducing me to families and easing an otherwise awkward interview with a stranger. One woman Slick introduced me to, for years had held the key to Rosa's story.

During the summer, Slick and his hard working wife, Marceline, ran Slick's Court. The wings of the motel made a courtyard in the center of which were several tall shade trees. Beneath the trees were several tables and chairs surrounded by rose bushes and flowers. After deer hunting season ended in October, Slick and Marceline closed the motel for the winter and retired to their home behind the motel.

Slick Bryant sat in his green golf cart watering the lawn as I walked up. The old man clutched the nozzle with both hands with difficulty. Several fingers were missing from each hand. He wore a T-shirt, his thin gray hair brushed back and gold wire rim glasses sat wisely on his thin nose. A day's stubble had sprouted on his face and neck, and you couldn't help but notice that Slick's legs were missing from just above the knee.

I recall one evening. Slick and I were going through several photo albums. He grinned broadly when we came to a photo taken twenty years earlier. Slick was standing on his long legs, holding a giant fish up with both hands, grinning like a fool, his hair still thick and dark. I could see he was proud of the great fish, and I think proud, too, for me to see him as he was once. The years had come and his legs had gone, and his body had grown smaller the way an old man's body does. I never asked about his legs. Someone said circulation in his legs got so bad, they were amputated. During our many meetings I never heard Slick complain of his loss nor mention it. I admired his courage. He was always joking, always witty, always glad to see you and help you if he could. Whenever I visited him, there was always someone there to talk with him; he had many friends. Slick was able to make people feel comfortable with his own great loss, never causing people to pity him. It seemed everybody in Bridgeport knew Slick; he was well liked and respected. At this writing, Slick's been dead about four months.

Slick Bryant had a large collection of Bodie papers which he had rescued from someone's trash heap. Aware of their historical value, he had bundled them up and carried them home. The papers were now in the vault of the Assessor's office. Slick's son, Dan Bryant, kept them there for protection. Dan had the early papers photographed and they were now on microfilm.

The newspapers were from the *Bodie Miner Index*, 1881-83. I was free to search the papers if I wanted. But there would be no point. Crippled as he was, Slick had plenty of time to read and reread the Bodie papers. He assured me that he never came across anything regarding Rosa May. I was disappointed but that was that.

But the interviews I had with Slick, and the picture he painted of the Bodie he knew seventy years ago, were worth as much as anything I might have learned from the old Bodie newspapers. Born so late in the last century, Slick never knew Rosa May but he remembered Ernest Marks and Billy Owens. In those days they referred to Marks' bar as Marks' Saloon. Like others, Slick recalled Marks was crippled and walked with a cane. He couldn't remember much else about him.

Billy Owens was the Bodie Justice of the Peace and the town's undertaker. Slick remembered Billy as a small man, and well liked. Outside of Ella Cain's story, he had never heard of Marks and Owens fighting over Rosa. Nor did he recall hearing about a pneumonia epidemic that killed Rosa and others. He assured me, pneumonia, as well as several other diseases, claimed many lives in the early days.

Slick was raised in Bridgeport but often visited Bodie with his father, becoming friends with many of the camp's families. The first time he went to Bodie was about 1908; Slick was nine. His first memory of Bodie was watching forty or fifty burros meandering down the road, each loaded with a quarter cord of wood. The Chinese had harvested pinon pines from the hills outside Bodie. They sold the wood to the townspeople, but their best customer was the Standard Mill which consumed twenty to thirty cords a day. The Standard later converted to electrical energy causing the Chinese woodcutters to lose their means of living, forcing them to move elsewhere. These woodcutters lived in wood camps several miles from Bodie and in Chinatown at the north end of town, west of Main Street. The houses of prostitution were in Chinatown which Bodie was never without.

The Standard was a twenty-stamp mill. Its job was to pulverize gold ore which was then amalgamated with mercury to draw out the gold. Compared to Virginia City's Consolidated Mill, which had eighty stamps, Bodie's Standard Mill was a baby. Yet Slick vividly remembered how the pounding of one stamp shook the entire town and the roar of the mill sounded like cannon fire. The Standard Mill ran continually. The townspeople were sure to awaken if its pounding stopped in the night for the Mill was the heart of their little community. When the Standard did not work, the men did not work. There would be no money to pay the grocer, the butcher, the shoe clerk. Bodie was completely dependent on its mines. The town eventually folded because the milling of low grade ore became unprofitable.

Bodie's Main Street stretched north and south. To the east was Bodie Bluff, and running south from the bluff was Silver Hill where other mines were located. Both sides of Main Street had the usual wooden buildings with high false fronts, all freshly painted bright white. East and west of Main there were the many cottages where miners and their families lived. The houses were small and without insulation. They were heated by wood burning stoves; kerosene lanterns provided light. A tank was attached to the kitchen stove where water was heated for bathing. Water was piped into the kitchen sink. Outhouses were as much a part of life as milk and butter. Some of the miner's cottages and various businesses had electricity after 1912, brought to Bodie by long distance transmission from Green Creek, about fifteen miles away.

In 1908, Slick figured Bodie must have had a population of about a thousand, served by several businesses. (Emil Billeb, author of *Mining Camp Days*, arrived in Bodie in 1908 as a young man, and estimated that there were no more than three hundred people.)

There were a number of saloons, Slick remembered three: Marks', Maestretti's and Seller's. There was a brewery run by an Irishman, John McKenzie. McKenzie's saloon faced Main Street and the brewery was behind the saloon. McKenzie's beer is supposed to have been very good, going for 5 cents a pony schooner, a small mug of beer.

In winter, the saloon keepers harvested ice from a reservoir up on Bodie Bluff. They stored the ice underground in sawdust for use in summer.

There were several general merchandise stores: Cecil Burkhams, Bill Reading's, Harvey Boone's and Tom Moyle's. Two butcher shops, one run by Clarence Wedertz, and the City Market, with meat carvers Donnely and Eli Johl, who married Lottie, from the red light district.

There were two hotels: the Occidental and the U.S. and several boarding houses. The hotels had bars and reasonable meals. Many bachelor miners lived in the boarding houses.

Men and women wore hats. A hat for a man was an absolute must and he wouldn't be caught without one. Women wore long dresses and had their hair pinned up neatly.

During Bodie's long winters, dances were held at the Miner s Union Hall. Slick's band often played at these. Bodie was without a library or the customary opera house. Families most often entertained friends at home.

In summer, Booker Flat, a large field on the south edge of town, was often used for picnics and baseball games. The Bodie baseball team played teams from Tonopah, Hawthorne, Bridgeport and other nearby towns. The teams took turns traveling by horse and wagon the many miles between their towns for the pleasure of heated competition.

The Bodie Slick knew as a kid, was a small town. There was one school for all grades and two churches, the Methodist and the Catholic. Many families were large and worked hard to subsist on the $4 a day miners made risking their lives in dangerous shafts.

With the town so small, everyone knew each other and helped one another in times of need. By today's standards, Bodie's townspeople were poor, but for the time, the small shanties teeming with children were quite common.

My interview with Slick took up the morning and part of the afternoon. Slick suggested I speak with Stuart and Sadie Cain who lived next door.

Sadie and Stuart were born in Bodie in 1891 and were raised in the camp. Stuart was the son of Jim Cain, Bodie banker and mining man. Because Stuart and Sadie were older and grew up in Bodie, Slick thought they could help me.

Stuart Cain met me at the door. At eighty-four, he had a remarkably boyish face with hazy blue eyes. I introduced myself and explained what I was doing.

Stuart smiled when I mentioned Rosa May but said nothing. I was told Stuart could be talkative about his home town or quite reticent. Today he was reticent. At another time, I spoke with his wife Sadie, who had a marvelous memory and was willing to talk. Sadie was one of few who had seen Rosa May alive.

I went back to Slick's and explained what had happened. He smiled. I thanked Slick for his help and said I'd write him when I got back south. He wished me luck, and we shook hands.

I headed out of Bridgeport on Highway 182, went through some mountains, crossed the Nevada state line, then down into the desert. Near Lucky Boy pass, I caught Highway 22 and turned north toward Yerington, Nevada. Markham Trailkill and Mrs. Bell lived in Yerington. I was told they could give me information about Bodie and Rosa May.

Yerington is a small town in Smith Valley. Like Bridgeport, the Walker River runs through the valley making it green with plenty of good grazing for sheep and cattle ranchers. Though a small town, Yerington is a metropolis compared to Bridgeport.

I found Markham Trailkill's place easily. He lived in a rambling two story boarding house for retired folks. I climbed the stairs, walked down a dark musty hall and knocked on Trailkill's door. He wasn't in. I walked back to the lobby and asked around for Trailkill. An elderly friend said I'd find him at a bar and casino on Main Street.

Markham Trailkill was sitting at an empty blackjack table. His newspaper was spread across the green felt. He was a gray headed fella in his seventies and wore glasses. He was friendly and over a couple beers we talked about Bodie and Rosa May.

Markham Trailkill told me the strangest story I ever heard about Rosa May and one I've never heard since. Yes, he said, Rosa May was buried in the outcast cemetery. She had died as Ella Cain had said, during what Trailkill called a "black pneumonia" epidemic. Black pneumonia killed within twenty-four hours. A miner would be sitting beside you one day and be dead the next.

Trailkill believed Rosa May died while helping miners and that she was buried outside the fence. However, according to Trailkill, in time people recognized the errors of their ways, repented, went back to the cemetery, dug up Rosa May and reburied her in the regular cemetery! Markham Trailkill told me this with a straight face and in all sincerity. I smiled; it was a hard tale to swallow.

Trailkill never knew Rosa May. He was born and raised in Yerington and worked one winter out in Bodie. Because of his more distant relationship with the camp, I doubted his story.

I left Yerington and drove out of town to the ranch where Mrs. Bell lived. Just before the ranch, I made my way through a throng of cattle being herded down a country road.

Mrs. Bell, then in her mid-nineties, lived in a mobile home on her son-in-law's ranch. She was the oldest woman I'd yet interviewed, silver haired, thin, dark wrinkled skin, cloudy eyes; and because of her senility, the most difficult to communicate with.

I spoke with Mrs. Bell for an hour about Bodie and Rosa May. She frequently apologized for her memory which was failing her. At this time, I believed Mrs. Bell was perhaps my last chance to learn something substantial about Rosa's life through old-timers. She was born during Bodie's boom. I believed I would not find anyone older than her.

Between her failing memory and her fading in and out of our conversation, Mrs. Bell gave me a few gems. She remembered Marks. She called him the Old Jew. He ran a saloon on the east side of Main, a block south of Jim Cain's bank. He also lived in a little cottage near the Bells, east of Main, behind the row of businesses. She remembered Marks as a man the children chased and gave trouble.

She remembered Rosa May. She said Marks was good to her and gave her gifts. He had "helped her out," she said.

She remembered seeing Rosa May a few times but "good women" never had anything to do with such girls. Prostitutes kept to themselves and lived in the north end in Chinatown. This was all she remembered. She apologized and faded away. I regret I did not speak with her again. On a good day she may have remembered more. Mrs. Bell died shortly after my visit.

As I left Mrs. Bell's, the clouds above Smith Valley had

gathered and grown somber. They poured torrents on the roads as I drove away. I listened to the splashing of my wheels in the rain as I left Yerington and headed toward Carson City.

The interview with Mrs. Bell was somewhat disheartening. I had come so close to learning something substantial about Rosa's life, but missed it. Now the hope of learning anything more from old-timers was fading. I was tired, too, from five days on the road driving all over hell asking strangers questions, and living out of my car. I wished I'd begun this search several years earlier before many of the old-timers had died. I would have had better luck.

I questioned whether or not I was wasting my time in this bazaar search. Again I felt a strange presence of someone or something in the car. What did it want? I was doing the best I could and I was tired. This was crazy. Perhaps, this someone or something was leading me on, helping me to find what it wanted me to find. We would see.

I planned to make it to Carson City by evening but I was tired of driving, and stopped in Gardnerville, twenty miles south. I had promised myself I wouldn't waste money on motels, but I succumbed to the need for a hot shower and a good night's rest. It was worth the money. I slept until eleven the next morning.

The next day I planned to go through public records in Carson City and Virginia City seeking information about Rosa May, Marks and Emma Goldsmith. According to Ella Cain, Rosa May had worked in brothels in both towns. I was guessing, but I figured Emma Goldsmith also came from this area before moving on to Bodie. I was hoping to find evidence that Rosa and Emma had owned houses of prostitution in Carson and Virginia City. I believed my chances were slim, but worth a try. Prostitutes seldom owned property, and very often madams did not own their houses.

From envelopes addressed to Rosa May in the Bodie Museum and from Ella Cain's story, I knew that Rosa May had lived at No. 1 Ormsby Street, Carson City and at 18 South D Street, Virginia City. If Rosa had not owned houses at these addresses, I hoped to learn who had.

Before searching Carson City records, I drove up and down Ormsby Street, now called Curry, admiring the huge cottonwoods that shaded the broiling street. The redlight district ran along Ormsby Street for several blocks. I was searching for No. 1 Ormsby Street. Frank Balfe had told me Carson City's remaining houses of prostitution were torn down several years ago.

I later learned No. 1 Ormsby Street would have been at the corner of King and Ormsby Streets. There were several reasons why this would have been a good location for a brothel.

For one, the Nevada State Legislature met only a block away on Carson Street, the main thoroughfare, along which were many businesses and hotels.

Secondly, the Virginia and Truckee Railroad depot was only seven blocks north at Caroline and Carson Streets. The United States Mint at Carson was right across from the train depot.

A brothel at King and Ormsby streets, then, was in the middle of the business district through which many men moved. Nevada legislators, train travelers, mint workers and men who worked at the Empire mills, several miles away, were likely customers.

I spent the morning and part of the afternoon in the Carson Courthouse searching land and death records for Rosa May, Emma Goldsmith and Ernest Marks. As with Mono County records, names were not alphabetized which made an easy job tedious.

A search of records from 1868 to 1901 found nothing. I was disappointed but that was that.

I drove up Carson Street crowded with summer travelers. I bought ice and food at a market, parked in the shade and devoured cold, sweet and sour plums and nectarines. My eyes were tired from searching faded records for several hours. After six days on the road alone, the search had become wearisome. I had learned a little more about Rosa May and Bodie, but not as much as I had hoped. I had no idea at the time that it would take me another three years to finish what I had begun. All I knew then was that I was tired, hot and hungry. I would search Virginia City records and then drive five hundred miles back to Riverside.

From Carson City you head east on U.S. Highway 50. About ten miles from Carson a road sign points north to Gold Hill and Virginia City. The land out here is fiercely dry and barren, covered by the ever present sagebrush and rabbit brush.

The road up to Virginia City winds through Gold Canyon, where gold and silver were discovered in 1859 causing the mining camps of Gold Hill and Virginia City to sprout. The two mining camps, a mile apart but working the same Comstock Lode, prospered for twenty years, the most profitable period 1873-79, the boom years.

In 1879 when Bodie boomed, Virginia City began losing her population of twenty thousand. As with the death of all mining camps, the lack of rich ore drove the money hungry souls elsewhere. It has been said that there never was a mining camp as grand as Virginia City and never will be one like it again. Virginia City's mines poured out hundreds of millions of dollars which helped the Union win the Civil War and established San Francisco as a major city.

As you drive up Gold Canyon, you read the tourist signs, all freshly painted with bright summer colors. The signs tell of Virginia City's past glory, of her most well known citizen, Mark Twain, and various saloons, mine tunnels and famous houses you can visit.

Up the steep canyon you pass a small cluster of houses, huge caverns and piles of golden sand. This is Gold Hill. A hundred years earlier Gold Hill had five to seven thousand citizens, throngs of saloons, hundreds of buildings and a newspaper. They are all gone.

The canyon gets steeper, you reach a switch-back, the car lugs, and finally you lunge over the crest, then down and your on C Street, Virginia City's main street.

Virginia City is built on the side of a barren mountain, once called Sun Mountain but known today as Mount Davidson. Streets running horizontally across the mountain are lettered, the highest is A Street. The poorest people lived farther down the mountain nearer to the mines and the horrible noise from the mills.

The mines are scattered about the mountain, the most profitable were located below D Street. The huge piles of earth and stone the miners dug out so long ago are here for the tourist to marvel at. But the hoisting works, the stamp mills, smoke stacks and mine buildings that once covered this area are gone and the area seems strangely deserted. The mining companies salvaged their equipment when they were done with Virginia City.

The Virginia City red light district was on D Street and ran for several blocks near the train depot. It was at 18 South D Street that Rosa once lived. I looked for the address but was disappointed to find all but one of the cribs gone. A bronze marker told of the district's active days.

I spent the afternoon in the Virginia City courthouse searching the heavy indexes for traces of Rosa May, Ernest Marks, and Emma Goldsmith. Because of Virginia City's greater success there were more indexes and more names, none alphabetized. I didn't finish work until the clerk was ready to shut her doors. The search proved fruitless. I was ready to go home.

Discouraged and tired but not defeated. On my way back to Riverside I interviewed three more old-timers and got lucky. In Lee Vining I spoke with Mrs. Katie Bell who had lived in Bodie. She was in her seventies.

Katie Bell never knew Rosa May but she had heard about her. She said Rosa May was a good hearted woman who helped the poor and low whenever she could. That was all Katie knew. She believed her brother, Richie Conway, whom I had tried to track down in Bishop, would know more. In Bishop there was also Anna McKenzie who had lived in Bodie. Anna might know something.

I zipped down to Bishop and this time Richie Conway was home. He was a ruddy faced old man, very warm and friendly. Richie Conway explained, very simply, that he had seen Rosa May when he was about seven years old. Born in 1895, this would make the time around 1902. Richie had delivered milk to her in the red light many times. He remembered her as a dark haired, middle aged woman. She was big hearted, he said, and never let anyone go hungry. Richie believed that she had had a large funeral.

He remembered times as a kid when his dad took him into the saloons where the red light girls were. The girls would pick little Richie up, set him on the bar and say, "Give him a drink; give him a drink."

That was all he could remember. He wished he could tell me more but he wasn't about to invent any tall tales. I believed him.

I was surprised to learn Rosa May was alive in 1902. Pleased with the news, I rushed over to Anna McKenzie for my last interview.

Anna McKenzie was born in Bodie in 1896. Her grandmother ran a two story brick boarding house in Bodie next to the Odd Fellows Hall. Anna's husband, Mervin McKenzie, dead several years, was a cousin of Bill Glenn's, whom I had the interviewed by letter.

Anna wished Mervin was alive. She said that he could have told me more about the Bodie red light and Rosa May. After all, it was men who knew about those things. Anna remembered that the Bodie prostitutes seldom came uptown. Instead, they phoned for deliveries of groceries, ice and beer. Anna's husband, Mervin, had delivered groceries to "those women."

The red light girls kept to themselves and were well ordered. Anna recalled that they seemed kind hearted. When a miner died, it was common custom for the prostitutes to take up a collection and offer the money anonymously to the miner's family.

Anna saw Rosa May once. Anna was twelve or fourteen at the time which would have made it 1908-10. She thought that Rosa was a quiet woman who kept to herself.

As a child, she also remembered seeing Lottie Johl, an ex-prostitute. After Lottie died Anna heard that Jim Cain bought Lottie's house.

In 1916, Bodie was slowing down. John McKenzie sold his brewery and saloon and left town. The red light girls were all gone by 1917 and it seemed to Anna that Rosa May must have died before this. She could not recall hearing of Rosa's death nor news of her funeral.

In parting, Anna offered the name of Guy McInnis, a man in his mid-nineties who was a bookkeeper for Cecil Burkham, who owned a store in Bodie and operated a stage between Bodie and Hawthorne. Anna believed Mr. McInnis was the oldest survivor from Bodie. He was nearly blind and lived in Hawthorne, Nevada.

I was glad to have found two people who had seen Rosa May, and to learn that Rosa May had lived as late as 1910. This would make research easier.

I had not found an intimate acquaintance of Rosa's, but Richie and Anna were a beginning. I drove home happy.

A month later I made another trip to the Bridgeport-Bodie area for more interviews. I hoped to find Rosa May's letters which were auctioned off in 1934 when Billy Owens died. You may recall that his property was bought by a certain B.C. Honea. From Slick Bryant I learned that a Honea ran a motel in Lee Vining.

In Lee Vining I discovered that a Briscoe Charles Honea had died several years earlier. His grandson, also named Briscoe, knew nothing about the Rosa May letters but he showed me the house his grandfather bought at the Bodie auction which was moved to Lee Vining. He also gave me the address of Chloe Clay, Honea's daughter, who might know something about the letters.

I had more luck. When I returned to Bridgeport, Slick Bryant introduced me to Helen Evans, Ella Cain's daughter. Helen Evans, then in her early seventies, was eager to help me. Asking if she knew anything about the Rosa May letters, she said, "Oh yes, I have twenty or thirty of them at my home in Pasadena." I was astonished.

It was Ella Cain, Helen's mother, who had bought Rosa May's trunk at the 1934 auction when Billy Owens died. The trunk contained Rosa May's clothing, photographs and letters.

Helen Evans summered in Bridgeport and wintered in Pasadena. I was free to review Rosa May's letters when she returned to Pasadena in October or November.

After a two month search I had finally found documents through which I might learn the truth about Rosa May's life.

68

Chapter 8

Hollywood. I set aside the Rosa May research. I was back in Southern California and ready to begin recording our album—the Big Dream.

Before the Mammoth gig, Kevin and I had met record producers who owned a recording studio in Pasadena. They had had one big hit record and they were looking for another. Supposedly, we were one of the acts they believed could put them back on the charts. They had listened to a demo (demonstration) tape of thirty of my songs and felt the material was strong. They wanted us to record an album. The producers would market the album to a large label. If things went as planned, the album would be distributed throughout the country, and with enough air-play bolstering sales, there was a chance I would become a wealthy young songwriter.

As is often the case in the music business, things didn't turn out as we hoped. The producers offered us a contract, fourteen pages of legal mumbo-jumbo. After deciphering the document with the help of Webster's dictionary, I discovered the contract was a sham, vague and tricky. It would leave us with a stack of bills that would take us years to pay, and tie up my copyrights for years. There would be no album, not now, not with these guys.

I had moved into an apartment in Pasadena; it seemed the place to live. We were recording our album in Pasadena and singing three nights at a club. Helen Evans also lived in Pasadena. I was eagerly awaiting her return so I could read the Rosa May letters.

We performed in Pasadena for several months at a posh, new restaurant, where valets swiftly hid customer's cars in the restaurant's vast parking lot. It was a strange gig. The owner hid us in a dark corner of the bar; customers ripped the hammers out of my piano and spilled drinks on the keys and woodwork. Patrons were rich and rude, and the thick cigarette smoke was nauseating.

One night matters came to a head. The owner gave us

hell about something and I told him to take a hike. He fired us. I could have cared less. I was tired of bars.,

I earned a living playing bars, but it was a was getting me nowhere as a songwriter. It was time to make the rounds with my songs in Hollywood.

I stopped singing in bars and tried to earn living some healthier way. My savings was gone and I started looking for work.

To hustle my songs in Hollywood during the day, I would need a part-time night job. That limited jobs.

I was broke when I finally landed a bartending job at a pizza place. I was so hard-up, I lied to get the job. I told the manager I was married and my wife was expecting. A gray haired, middle-aged man, he knew about babies and bills and gave me the job. Now and then he asked about my wife and I had to lie to him again. There's a moral in there somewhere. I didn't like lying but I had needed the job desperately.

So here I was, a college graduate, professional musician, struggling songwriter, stumbling historical researcher—pouring beer and soda for minimum wage and grateful to have the job. I worked from four to midnight, and hustled my songs in the day.

Hollywood, the fabled town of dreams and illusions. My plan was to interest a publisher in my songs. A publisher's job is to find hit songs. If a publisher believes a song will be profitable, he offers you a contract. Publisher and songwriter split the profits.

Publishers shop their songs to artists, producers and recording companies, trying to get their songs recorded. Producers look for hit songs for the artists they produce. The producer pitches the songs to non-writing artists. If the artist believes in the song, he records it. The song is then manufactured into CD's and tapes. The recorded song is marketed and distributed by the artist's record company to radio stations and stores throughout the country and the world. If the artist is fortunate, the record company's promotion people get behind the song and push it. The marketing and promotion of an artist and his record, determines whether or not a song becomes a hit.

I had recorded a demo of thirty songs I believed were

marketable. From this tape, I selected four of the strongest and transferred them to cassette tapes. On the cassette label I wrote the names of the songs, my name and phone number.

I wrote songs to express myself. I tried to write memorable melodies combined with sincere lyrics, from the heart, plain and simple.

On the West Coast, those in the business know their livelihood comes from the young songwriters on the street who are eventually discovered and become money-makers. Therefore, some publishers let guys from the street make appointments to show two or three of their best songs.

But even in Hollywood, the number of publishers with such an open door policy is small. Most often a writer must mail his songs in on a CD or cassette. Publishers hire song screeners to listen to the demos.

Each Monday morning, I called publishers and tried to set up appointments to see people. I had to call early and I had to call Monday or I wouldn't be seeing anyone that week and a week of hustling would be wasted.

I showed up at these meetings with my guitar case in hand, with a cassette demo and a typed copy of lyrics for each song. I shook the man's hand, took my guitar out of the case, and pick in hand, sang the songs for the song screener. If the screener liked the song, he let me continue. If he didn't, he told me to stop and go on to the next song.

Most of the big Hollywood publishers have their offices in the several high-rise buildings on the 6400 block of West Sunset. You walk into the expansive lobbies of these buildings, find the directory and locate the floor and room of the publisher with whom you have an appointment. When you reach the floor, the elevator dumps you into a carpeted hallway. There, you wonder quite nervously what you're doing and whether you're a songwriter after all. This is the first time you've met with a publisher and you're about to have the first professional judgment of your material. And to put it honestly, you're scared out of your wits.

You walk down one hallway to the left of the elevator only to discover you're on the wrong side of the building. You go back to the elevator, cross over to the next hallway and find Zeke Publishing. You knock, walk in and find yourself in a small reception area with thick carpet, leather couch, various music industry magazines on the table, and a pretty receptionist who asks you who you are and what you want.

You explain you have an appointment with so and so. She tells you he'll be out shortly. You sit on the couch feeling quite jittery. Mouth dry, you check and re-check to see if you've brought everything. You've got the right tape for the right publisher. You've got the right lyric sheets. Your guitar is tuned; you're ready to go.

For twelve years you've been putting words and music together. You believe you're a good songwriter with strong material, but you're still nervous. You don't know why, but yes you do. This guy's about to pronounce judgement on your songs in about five minutes. These are your babies, the basis for your dreams, your hopes, that precious part of you that doesn't want to get crushed. You want this guy to like your songs, and if he doesn't, it's bad news.

The door opens, and a guy your age introduces himself. He's dressed in jeans and a T-shirt but he's still a businessman no matter how laid-back he looks. You smile, shake his hand, try to talk confidently.

He leads you through the door, down a hall to his office. His office is small; there might be an out of tune piano on one wall, a large desk with tapes and papers and lead sheets scattered across it. He might have a few posters or pictures of artists tacked to the wall, artists for whom he handles the publishing.

He sits down behind his desk. He wants to know about you. How long have you been in Hollywood? Have you ever been published? What's your track record, any Hit songs? How long have you been writing songs, etc. He eyes you with a clinical coldness. He doesn't have time to waste.

He asks if you want to play your tapes on his machines on the rack behind his desk. No, you'd rather sing them yourself.

So now it's all yours. You've got to prove to this guy that you're a great songwriter and your songs will make him and his company a lot of money.

You unlatch the metal snaps on your guitar case, take your guitar out, reach in your pocket for a pick, sit back down and closing your eyes, you try to go back to that special moment when you first started writing this song. Though the feeling is gone, once you open your mouth and begin to sing, strumming the chords of your song, there it is again, the magic you felt as you wrote the song, that night very late when the music began to sing and through that mysterious creative processes of mind and heart, with God's gift and a lot of hard work, you brought the song out of you into the world of sound. And now you're not thinking about this guy or what he thinks, and the jittery feeling's leaving your stomach, replaced with a lovely warmth, the warmth of your love and your belief in your child: your song.

You finish singing, open your eyes, and your eyes are meeting his, and you see his eyes have softened and he's smiling. You want to know what he things. You're talented, he says. It's a strong song, but it's not a Hit and he needs Hits. But he relaxes now; he knows you're not some fool off the street who picked up a guitar six months ago and thinks he's a songwriter. And in his knowing that you've got something, you begin to relax.

He wants to hear more, so you sing a couple more songs. He's impressed, you're a good songwriter, but the songs just aren't Hit songs. He wants a tape, so you hand him a cassette with your copyright seal, name and address.

That's all that can happen today. You walk out of his office feeling ambivalent. You're not a failure; you're not a success. You're not in nor out; you're just hanging, and the rent is due and you're not a Hit songwriter yet and you're worried.

You have an appointment with another guy an hour later. You hang around the street for an hour and then climb up another building to another publishing rep where the same scene is acted out. And the next day you see someone else, and the next day someone else and they all say the same: you're a good songwriter, you've got strong songs, but they're not Hit songs and you try not to believe them.

After a few weeks you've met with a number of reps,

about all you can get in and see. The news spreads fast among the publishers that a new writer is in town and he's good but he's not hot yet.

After meetings I drove home to Pasadena. The interviews and excitement wore me out. I grabbed something to eat, laid down and wondered whether or not I would ever sign with a publisher.

Days I was unable to meet with publishers, I spent writing and taping new songs, and trying to write the Rosa May novel, which was not going well.

At the Pasadena Library, I gathered and read volumes on Bodie, Virginia City, California and Nevada history, and prostitution. Slowly I was getting a feel for Rosa's era, and how prostitutes fit into the scheme of early California and Nevada life.

I also spent many hours at the Los Angeles Museum of Natural History. There I searched and found early photos of Bodie and Virginia City. I also checked early City Directories and Pacific Coast Directories for Rosa May hoping to discover where she was living and when.

John Cahoon, L.A. Museum curator, was very helpful. He made me aware of AA. Forbes, a Bishop photographer who visited Bodie in the late 1890's up until 1910 or so. During his summer stays at Bodie, Forbes shot a slew of Bodie photographs, one of which is included in the photo section. The photo is an excellent shot showing the Bodie red light district and Rosa May's house.

In addition, John Cahoon informed me of the Burton Frasher photograph collection at the Pomona Library. Burton Frasher accompanied Carl Parcher Russell, a writer, to Bodie in the fall of 1927. Frasher's 1927 photos of the Bodie cemetery eventually led me to the discovery of Rosa May's actual gravesite.(See photo section.)

I still had not located any documents regarding Rosa's death. In efforts to do so, I contacted the Methodist and Catholic churches, the only churches that had established themselves in Bodie. The search of these records took many months, and proved fruitless.

Afterward, I tried to locate families of priests and ministers who had served in Bodie, hoping they might have passed down a journal or log that would mention Rosa May's death. This, also, proved fruitless.

However, my correspondence with the Methodist Church put me in contact with Will Ralph, Methodist Archivist at Berkeley.

Ralph visited Bodie in 1961, at which time he took a picture of Rosa's grave. (Photo section.)At that time a wooden post and sign marked Rosa's gravesite prior to Louis Serventi's marker.

In the LA Museum library I came across Carl Parcher Russell's article, "The Bodie That Was," published in the November, 1929 issue of *Touring Topics*, later *Westways* magazine. Included in the article were some of Burton Frasher's photos. During Russell's visit to Bodie for the article, Russel met and interviewed Earnest Marks. In the following excerpt, Russell calls Marks, "Smith," and refers to Rosa May as "Rosemary." Speaking of Maiden Lane, the Bodie red light district, Russell explains the relationship between Rosa May and Ernest Marks:

Here "Rosemary" reigned for a time and with one, whom we shall call Smith, maintained a noted business of prostitution and gambling.

Their partnership was quite as successful as some of the mining combinations on the mountainside above their den. Wealth flowed into their household, and Rosemary sported huge jewels and rich raiment. But Rosemary died. We may believe that the dapper Smith grieved, but he was not overcome. He took unto himself another mistress. Partner number two fell short of Rosemary in business ability and sincerity toward Smith. At an opportune time she absconded and with her went a goodly share of the cash assets of the business, as well as the best jewels and furs left by the late Rosemary. A manager of the proper philosophic attitude was essential to the Maiden Lane branch of the business and Smith accepted a third partner. Like her predecessor, she laid hands upon more than a paltry of the accumulated wealth, and the cream of the remaining Rosemary jewels. How many times this drama of chance-taking and loss was enacted only Smith can tell. He is not apt to be found in a reminiscent mood so far as these bits of per-

sonal history are concerned. I met him at the door of a dilapidated li-
quor house on Main Street, and almost at once he displayed to me what
I presume is his last jewels of those days o half a century ago. Within
the old saloon he fries his bacon and makes his bed, where once milled
hundreds of miner's feet. I discovered that his roulette wheel abides
with him still.

Absolutely alone on the street of deserted business establish-
ments, he impressed me as a most pathetic individual. Slumped down
as he was in an old saloon chair, his withered little form seemed to need
more than the feeble autumn sunshine that fell upon it. As I talked to
him, his slender, agile fingers played about his vest pockets, and pres-
ently he drew forth a gold match case. "That's Bodie ore! Look at it.
More gold than quartz. And there is more of it in the old hill yonder.
I'll stay till she booms again." One wall of this watch case was formed
by a beautifully polished section of very rich quartz. The natural de-
sign made by the gold veins imprisoned within the quartz formed an
"R."

Here was Ernest Marks, nearly fifty years after Bodie's
boom drew him, utterly alone, unwilling to speak of his earlier
years with Rosa. As Russell and Marks talked, neither knew
Marks would shortly join Rosa May on the sage covered slopes
above the town.

Though it was forty-seven years since Russell published
his article, I tried to find him. He was dead and had not left
behind notes of his 1927 interview with Marks.

Chapter 9

Helen Evans returned to Pasadena in mid-November. The morning we were to meet, my VW finally gave up the ghost. I borrowed a car and made the meeting on time. I brought my notebook and a cassette recorder; Mrs. Evans did not want the letters to leave the house. I would have to read the letters aloud and tape them on the cassette. Afterward, I would transcribe the letters from tape.

Cordial and silver haired Helen Evans met me at the door and led me to her living room where we spoke briefly. She had set up a card table on top of which was a packet of letters. Understanding my eagerness, Helen left me and busied herself with the maid in the kitchen.

I opened the packet of letters and thumbed through them. There were about thirty letters. Holding the letters, I felt anxious, knowing in a moment, I would be reading letters that were written a hundred years ago and meant to be read only by Rosa May.

I spread the envelopes out on the table. Each letter was still enclosed in its envelope. The envelopes were of various colors: yellow, white, orange and baby blue. All bore the Wells Fargo and Co. insignia. Most were the green, three cent stamped envelopes I first saw at the Bodie Museum.

The envelopes, like those at the Museum, were neatly opened with a knife at the narrow, right end. As I took the letters from their envelopes, I noticed the paper was still white and crisp, as it must have looked on the day the letter was written. Kept in the envelopes away from air and sun all those years, the paper had not discolored. The rich black ink stood out clearly; the lines of the letters twisted fat and thin from the quill pens used long ago. The ornate writing was difficult to make out in places. Certain letters looked foreign and oddly shaped compared to today's handwriting.

It took me three hours to read through the letters. I read each letter silently, struggling to make out the more obscure words. When I was certain I knew what most of the letter said, I read the letter aloud and taped it on the cassette recorder. I made certain to note the date each letter was written, in what city, and, by whom.

When I got back to my apartment, I began transcribing the letters from the tape; this took several days.

The were twenty-five letters written by eight persons over a three and a half year period between September 27, 1876 and March 27, 1880. Most of the letters were addressed to Rosa in Carson and Virginia City. None were addressed to her in Bodie.

Of the twenty-five letters, four are addressed to Rosa in Virginia City. These include the earliest letter, September 27, 1876, and the latest, March 27, 1880. Three of these letters are addressed to Rosa at 18 South D Street, a brothel operated by Cad Thompson, a woman who ran various houses of prostitution on South and North D streets from the 1860's to the early 1890's.

The Virginia City red light district was on D Street, bounded on the south by Taylor Street. Union Street was the dividing line for addresses running north and south; addresses north of Union, were on North D Street.

Cad Thompson's brothel at 18 South D Street was on the west side of D, between Union and Taylor. Oddly enough, City Hall was in the same block. The Virginia and Truckee passenger depot was near Thompson's place, on the northeast corner of Union and D Street.

Eighteen letters over a one year period, from July 7, 1878 to August 15, 1879, were received by Rosa at various addresses in Carson City. Most of these letters were written by Ernest Marks, Rosa's lover, living at that time in Gold Hill. Rosa had various post office boxes in Carson City: numbers 2, 40 and 49. She also received letters at No. 1 Ormsby Street and in care of Jennie Moore, a black woman, age 54, who ran a house of prostitution on the northwest corner of Third and Ormsby.

The Carson red light district was on Ormsby Street, now called Curry. According to the June 9, 1875 issue of the *Carson Appeal*, the red light was restricted to Ormsby Street between Second and Fifth streets. However, knowing, that Rosa received letters at No. 1 Ormsby, which would have been at the corner of

King and Ormsby, one block north of fifth, it appears the red light ran from Second Street north along Ormsby as far as King Street. This made the Carson red light district four blocks long, as large as the Virginia City red light district.

Included in the letters, was a letter Rosa May had written which was returned to her. This letter proved invaluable when the letters were examined by handwriting analysts.

And finally, there was one pencil written note from Isaac Isaacs, a Virginia City clothing merchant who asked Rosa to meet him at his room after work, for, shall we say, a private entertainment.

The first reading of the letters was difficult because I did not know many common expressions of the era, nor did I know who were the various people mentioned in the letters, a total of thirty-six. Through use of City Directories, census and newspapers, I was able to identify most of the thirty-six.

For your convenience and better understanding, as I present each letter I explain common expressions of the era and identify people mentioned. This will help your first reading of the letters far more informative than mine.

I know of no other collection of letters written to a Western mining camp prostitute. I have decided to publish all twenty-five letters considering their historical value. I have placed the letters in chronological order and have kept the original spelling as I believe this reveals the writer's character. However, in some letters, I have created paragraphs and added periods for easier reading.

The first letter is from Laura Davenport and is addressed to Rosa May at 32 South D Street, Virginia City, Nevada:

Wednesday Afternoon
New York, Sept. 27th, 1876

My Dear Friend Rose,

I received your kind letter and was glad to hear from you once more and also that you have recovered from your chills and fever. I have heard before about that medicine being good and told Joe of it, but he is all go on quinnie [I believe she means quinine] *I tell him I guess it makes him feel good. I hope it doese.*

Rose I was to a wedding last night at the St. Stephens Church. The couple were real nice looking and the Bride was dressed very neat and pretty. The organ played the Wedding March when they were coming in and it sounded beautiful. The Bride's father brought her up to the altar and gave her away. This is the first time since I have been in New York that I ever seen a wedding or rather seen a couple married. It tis a kind of solemn thing after all.

I was a wishing that I was a good virtuous girl and it was Joe and me but no such good luck, but you can bet if I had my life to live over and knew as much as I do now, I would never do wrong. Well there is no use to look at the past, for that is gone long ago.

I met one of the old sewing women [prostitute] *the other day and she told me that Maggie Belmont was a coming on here after women. It is time for the Landladies* [madams] *to make their appearance from the South and all round.*

I don't know them girls you mention in your letter.I am glad that your are doing well, too and save some money and come back to New York and I want you to hold my baby and see it I think Rosa after all these years I am caught. [pregnant] *I am not fooling. I haven't been unwell* [had a period] *in two months, unless this month shows something and it tis most out now. I feel awfully worried about it, it may come out all right, I hope so.*

You want to know if we have joined the church, not exactly. Rose do you ever hear what has become of Sopky Post. I would really like to know. What is your Landlady name [she could mean, what is your prostitute alias, but more likely, what is your madam's name.] *I never of seen it in many a long day, God knows what has become of him, for I don't. Why don't you write to his last address. What was his last name I never knew.*

Rose just as soon as I get my new Black Silk Suit I am going to send you a good picture of me. You might let me have that one I had taken in Havana for I haven't got any that was taken so long ago of me and if anything should happen to you it would only fall into strangers hands. You might let me have it.

Well I haven't any more to write this time, the people that I board with is trying to sell out, so I can't tell what minute I shall have to change quarters so you had better direct to the Station.[Post office]

Good By a kiss Love From Your Friend
Mrs. Laura Davenport
Station Y Third Avenue
Ans. soon
Joe wished to be remembered to you
Excuse poor writing

From this letter it appears Rosa May had been in Virginia City for some time. From Laura's inquiries concerning Sopky Post, we know that Laura and Joe spent time in Virginia City before their recent return to New York. Rosa may have lived in New York, considering Laura's urging that she "try and save some money and come back to New York." That Rosa May was from the East instead of Paris as Ella Cain said, will be later be shown.

Though Rosa is doing well financially, she has suffered from chills and fever. We do not know what has caused the chills and fever. By September, Virginia City's nights were growing cold high in the mountains. The red light cribs were flimsy frame shacks which permitted wind and cold to easily enter. Most cribs were small one story buildings with a front and back room. The front room had a few chairs, perhaps a carpet, bureau, mirror, various pictures on the walls, and photos of loved ones. The back room consisted of a three-quarter size bed and a pot belly stove fed by wood or coal and used for cooking and heat. There was an outhouse behind the crib.

The flimsy cribs may have partly been the cause of Rosa's chills and fever. However, we know today that illness is not only caused by bacteria and viruses but also by various insecurities we face. A worrisome man's back begins to ache. An anxious girl develops ulcers. One wonders whether or not Rosa's chills and fever were caused by the isolation and precariousness of her work and life. Rosa's illnesses are mentioned by several writers in various letters.

For me, the most interesting and touching part of Laura's letter is the wedding she witnessed. Laura wistfully remarks that a wedding "is a kind of solemn thing after all," something she wished Joe and her had. She regrets her years as a prostitute and wishes she was a "good virtuous girl," but such possibilities are "gone long ago." Her father will never be giving her away.

Laura is afraid that she is "caught," pregnant. Pregnancy greatly complicated the prostitute's life. It caused her to lose her means of living for a time which caused troubles with her pimp. Such men even resented a woman's period, as a girl could not work. For Laura, pregnancy meant another responsibility.

Since this is the only letter we have of Laura's, we are left to wonder many things. Certainly, the details here do not point toward a happy ending for all concerned.

The photograph Laura mentions of Laura in her black silk suit, is very likely the photograph I first saw at the Bodie Museum, which was supposedly Rosa May. The woman in the photograph only resembles Rosa May, and she is wearing a black silk dress.

Interesting that Rosa asks if Laura and Joe have become members of the church. Many prostitutes were religious. Mexican prostitutes often had crucifixes nailed to their crib walls.

The next letter was written in San Francisco, December 12, 1876, by a man we will simply know as Jack.

My Own Darling Rose —

I presume you think I do not care much for you by allowing your kind note to remain so long unanswered. It is nothing but neglect Rose. I have thought of it several times but not having a right good show to ans. let it go until thinking you might become disgusted. I take this show to drop you a line — I see in your last [letter] your natural distrust of me shows up- I tell you darling that if stocks go up I would see my little one if only for a short time. You may think it in your minds eye or not- Wont you let me tell the truth once Rose? I think sometimes you mean what you say and its but fast for you to reciprocate — Speaking of that cane my dear as long as you keep it for yourself it will not hurt you- Again if stocks do ever go up I'll make it something better than a cane for you to remember me by.

What is the matter with Ophir [a large producing mine in Virginia City] *up there. They have knocked the d- h- out if it here- I*

hope business is good with your darling and that you are happy. If you'll believe me I'll think the world of little Rose
yours,
Jack

This short letter gives us our first clues about Rosa's character.

Jack, more than likely, was a customer of Rosa's while he was in Virginia City. There is a hint here that he may have been more to Rosa than a customer, by Jack's referring to Rosa as, "My Own Darling Rose." Whatever terms they were on, it appears Jack owes Rosa money. Prostitutes sometimes allowed customers to run tabs. Problems arose when customers lost money in stocks. Prostitutes were the last to receive what was owed.

Rosa has evidently sent Jack a "kind" reminder that it's time to pay up. His cane will not suffice for payment. Jack blames the drop in stocks both for his inability to pay Rosa and for failing to visit her.

It is important to note, that Jack, as other writers, refers to Rosa as "little Rose" or "little one," making it obvious that Rosa May was a small woman.

In Jack's letter we first come across Rosa's deep distrust of men. "I see in your last, your natural distrust of me shows up." Rosa had reasons to distrust Jack, as an analysis of his handwriting clearly showed. Rosa's involvement with unstable and untrustworthy men is a recurring theme throughout the letters. Her need to choose such men will be explained later.

"I think sometimes you mean what you say and it's but fast for you to reciprocate," hints that Rosa's kind note was also angry and demanding. Rosa's hot temper, her cutting tongue and impulsive nature is revealed here and in other letters.

The Ophir Mine was a large producing mine in Virginia City in 1876. "They have knocked the damn hell out of it here," refers to the manipulation of all Virginia City mining stocks by San Francisco stock brokers, who were called, "Bears."

In July, 1876, the Bears believed the price of Consolidated Virginia and California Mine stocks, the richest Comstock mines, were over priced. They suspected Mackay, Fair and Flood, mine owners, of unloading their own stocks.

In an effort to drive stocks down, the Bears, led by Keene, a broker, began a savage attack on the Consolidated Virginia and California stocks, disregarding the fact that these mines were breaking records in amounts of ore milled, resulting in great profits. In one month, March 1876, the mines produced $3,634,218! Stocks were worth the asking price.

But the Bears continued their attack, managing to drive stocks down, depressing the market. Con. Virginia stock dropped from $440 to $240 a share; the California from $90 to $65 a share.

With the Bonanza mine stocks driven down, other stocks fell, including the Ophir, which evidently Jack had bought into.

Some notes on Virginia City mines: their greatest yield was 1874-80, though the mines were worked from the 1800's to the present. In 1876 it was not known how far the great body of silver ore extended. As far as it had been explored, it was city blocks wide and deep. Some believed that the silver ore was inexhaustible.

By 1877, the extent of the ore was known. It was not inexhaustible. Though 1877 was the greatest year of production for the mines, it was ironically a year of economic depression and poverty for the citizens of Virginia City. Many miners lost jobs and were unable to feed their families.

From 1878 on, silver production in the Comstock mines dropped year by year and stock values fell with the decline.

The following is the first of the many letters written by Ernest Marks, Rosa's long time lover. This first letter was not written to Rosa, but to a prostitute we will simply know as Jennie. It's doubtful this is Jennie Moore, who ran a brothel in Carson at Third and Ormsby.

Whenever Marks refers to "the Doctor," he is speaking of his penis. The term reflects Marks' vanity, that his sexual prowess is capable of doctoring any woman's sexual needs. Ernest Marks was twenty-three when he wrote this letter.

Rolands Lake Tahoe
July 7, 1878

My Dear Jennie

Your two letters are at hand this day-as luck would have it I opened the dizy one first-it made me feel funny to see and you can't tell how quick I knew that you had been on a dizy spell but when I opened no. 2 Oh! how glad I was to see my darling was her self once more her dear lady likeself—

I have just arrived. The pop and gin and the medicine are here all o.k. and I now hope I shall be as sound as a roach [Marks may have had a venereal disease.] *I have had a very nice time since I left. I have caught a great many of the speckled beauties and had around 50 in a pen—the thing busted and let them out and for two or three days the wind blew so hard that I could not catch enough to eat- So today we left Camp Starvation as I called it. This week on the 4th I fished all day and only got enough to eat but I hope Monday I shall be able to get a lot to send home to Ed and Taylor so that my baby can also have a mess. I dont know how soon I will be able to write again. I shall try and be home as soon as I get well, if I don't get well I will come home for getting up at night to release the Dr. from a crooked posish is not what it is cracked up to be as it is rather colder here at night than it is in Virginia City but I just grin - Oh! such a grin—but it is not as bad as it was at home and my large left* [testicle?] *is a thing of the past thank the devil. I am writing this by the campfire, so you will excuse the bad writing.*

Peacock is at Emerald Bay. I saw him yesterday. I have seen one or two chances to give the Dr. a chance but he and I do not give it a thought. I suppose a great love of Jennie blinds us to everything else.

Tomorrow I shall go to the Glenbrook for provisions—I shall always write you at every opportunity. You can write me same as before and if I don't get them sooner I will later.

Old Tom is to much of a d—d fool to take any notice of-and if he is my friend let him conduct himself as such not like a sneak, his natural way of doing.

There was a woman said to me yesterday, "Don't you get lonesome when you have no ladies around. "Oh, yes " I said. I could be of no use to her [why?] *so I left. Dr. did not show any symptoms of wanting any and I was very glad to see he had not forgotten his Rosa.*

*I am getting as brown as I can make no...[Indecipherable]
and I have not shaved since I left you - I look rough so Mountain Jack
and Rich call me Wild Bill. I do get a little wild sometimes but quit
drinking from tonight till I am more your darling as of yore.*
    *[Indecipherable]... My sister said Ed's hair was all coming
out in spots. Ed said in his letter that it is no better. I am sorry if he has
taken a dose. All my paper is gone. I shall get more. I will see you in the
sweet by and by my love. With lots of love and kiss. I am your Ernie.*

Marks' rambling letter is confusing. If he and Rosa have
a relationship, why does he say, "I suppose a great love of Jennie
blinds us to everything else," and later say, "...I was very glad
to see that he [Marks' penis] had not forgotten his Rosa," It's
difficult to determine exactly what Jennie is to Marks.

That she is a prostitute, we can be certain and likely a
friend of Rosa's. Whether Jennie and Marks have something
going on behind Rosa's back, we do not knew. An analysis of
Marks' handwriting reveals that he had a tremendous sexual
appetite, the kind of man who was constantly thinking of sex,
and often frequented brothels. As for his fidelity, Marks was as
true as the wind.

Lake Tahoe is about fifteen miles west of Carson City,
high in the Sierra. It seems that Marks has a venereal disease
and has gone to the mountains to recuperate. His mentioning of
the arrival of medicine, "I shall try and be home as soon as I am
well," and "...my large left [testicle?] is a thing of the past," all
point to Marks having v.d. Knowing his sexual appetite, when
he says, "I could be of no use," to the lonely mountain woman,
makes one feel certain that Marks is temporarily out of commission.

According to statistics gathered by Eliot Lord and published in his, *Comstock Mining and Miners*, 1883, an extremely
well written and informative book about life in Virginia City,
venereal disease was the most frequently treated illness on the
Comstock.

From 1865 to 1880, the Storey County Hospital had
treated 731 cases of v.d., not including hundreds of cases not
reported or treated elsewhere. Virginia City never had a medi-

cal clinic where prostitutes could be examined and treated. Considering the large numbers of prostitutes and the lack of proper medical care and education, it is a wonder venereal disease did not prevail in epidemic proportions.

Ed, a friend of Marks who is often mentioned in his letters, seems also to have v.d. "My sister says Ed's hair was all coming out in spots. Ed said in his letter that it is no better. I am sorry if he has taken a dose."

The names mentioned here are often mentioned in Marks' letters. Peacock and Rich are friends. Old Tom, is most likely Tom Reynolds, who ran a hides and pelt store in Gold Hill and was a frequent customer of Rosa's.

Marks mentions his drinking problem here and throughout the letters. He was an alcoholic. Most men along the Comstock drank enormous quantities of liquor. There were a hundred saloons in Virginia City, thirty-seven in Gold Hill. After a time, most men could drink huge quantities and not feel it. The Comstock had Victorian customs; it was considered unmanly to lose control under the influence.

This letter proves that Marks and Rosa knew each other as early as July 7, 1878. They did not meet each other in Bodie as Ella Cain claims.

Another letter from Ernest Marks, his first to Rosa May:

Gold Hill
Dec. 20, 1878

Dearest One,

Many thanks for your loveing letter of the 19th. I always feel so happy when I hear from you. But so blue when I know I cannot come or be with my Rosa my baby — the time passes very slowly when you are not with me — I don't see any fun — and how, I miss my pet at night no one knows except poor me. I am still going hungry [without sex] and I suppose I will till I see my pet. It seems as though every man woman and child knew of you and I. I get it from some quarter every day. And it makes me feel so bad sometimes that I hardly know what to do. I feel very desperate just now any ways no money, no friends but one, be-

sides my baby.

I am thinking myself that I am going to lose my pay— it will be a $122 tonight. I am agoing up to see Tom about it to see if he got any letter from the president yet. If I don't get it I can't get my little one her presents as I had not enough to pay for them— but we still live in hope.

I took in the show last night and thought Tom was in for a bad scrape once while he was taking his girl home. That fellow is tough but Tom stood him off— But Donnie is afraid of Jack though she told him to keep away last night. If there had been a scrape I should have been into it as I think it is time someone else has a chance to do a little f—ing in this town beside the so called sports— I guess Jack will let Tom alone now as he had the worst of the bargain last night.

I hope you will be careful and not let yourself be bilked [cheated] *any more. Charles Boscowitz is a married man, as I am acquainted with his wife—or I may be mistaken it may be his brothers or someone else's wife of the same name but I rather think it is his, I am not certain but you will find it out soon enough if you don't know it now.* [Evidently Boscowitz cheated Rosa out of money. Marks may be hinting here, that if Boscowitz has a wife, Rosa could blackmail him, which was common.] *Don't you forget it I shall see without anyone knowing it that Dora hears of her Peter. Damn them, they would give me away if they could but I don't propose to break my baby's heart by going around with the dizy girls and boys. I am now good and keep away from them all. And good I shall be and save it all for my sweet so that I "Shall be able" when I meet her again—I hope it may be soon and I know you do.*

I saw Jim Breen on the street last night and he told me Mollie O'Neil had gone to Carson on the evening train. There was no love there. He was still in the street he said... [Marks loses his thoughts.]

Your bird is singing pretty as I write this. The old lady wanted to give him a name—but I told her that he would soon be gone—and then he would get a new name.

I am glad to think Em [Emma] *did not try my pet. I expect to hear if I get among the boys and girls that you had a lover but I won't believe it as I know my Rosie loves her baby don't you darling* [This may imply that Emma made a pass at Rosa. From here it would seem that Marks fears that Rosa has a lesbian lover, and perhaps has had one in the past. Prostitutes often turned to each other for affection, having been mauled by men day after day.]

I shall be off to see Tom soon—I guess Reynolds will be down about Christmas—so Oily Gammon tells me. With great love and a million kiss— I am your Erni.

Ernest Marks' first letter to Rosa May in Carson City, was written during an economic depression on the Comstock Lode. The end of the Great Bonanza was now in sight. Only the Bonanza mines were profitable and able to keep miners employed. The majority of the mines had closed down or had levied assessments on stock holders. Many miners were unemployed and grubbed for whatever work available to support their hungry families. Begging in the streets by widows and orphans was common. Two bit saloons became bit saloons; businesses went bankrupt or were forced to move elsewhere. The outlook for all was gloomy. The miners and merchants had put their complete trust in the mines. Once thought inexhaustible, the mines were now giving out. All were dismayed.

The question arises while reading Marks' letter, that if he missed Rosa as much as he says he does, why didn't he live in Carson City nearer to her? Or, why didn't he visit her more often? Carson City was a two hour train trip from Virginia City. The trip took so long because of the lengthy switch-backs down the mountains to Carson.

Marks did not visit Rosa more often perhaps for two reasons: one, he probably didn't have the train fare. Second, assuming Marks worked during the day, he would have had to visit Rosa at night, during Rosa's working hours. Not good for Rosa's business nor Marks' vanity.

In the first paragraph we learn that others know about Marks and Rosa. Marks is not happy about this. In fact, he's ashamed that people know that he is romantically involved with a prostitute. His shame reflects his guilt which often seeps from his letters. There is little doubt that men in the saloons he frequents have been razzing him about Rosa. "I get it from some quarter every day. And it makes me feel so bad sometimes that I hardly know what do."

The pay of a $122 Marks fears he may lose, was quite a sum considering miners made $4 a day for eight hours of grueling work, $20 a week, $80 a month, and $4 a day at this time was top money.

Marks was sexually obsessive and alcoholic. He hung around the red light dives and saloons with a group of men who befriended the local prostitutes. Some of these men were miners; others, pimps or men who lived off the earnings of prostitutes. Marks often refers to these as the "dizy girls and boys." "...I don't propose to break my baby's heart by going around with all the dizy girls and boys. I am now good and keep away from them all." Rosa evidently, knew that Marks hung around with other prostitutes and pimps when he was away from her. When he did so, she knew he drank and had relations with other prostitutes. Though Rosa bartered her body daily to many men, ironically she expected Marks to be monogamous, something of which he was incapable. His strong sexual appetite needed to be fed often and with many different women.

Though he defends himself here and claims that he is "now good," one can be certain, his recent celibacy will not last long.

Tom, most likely the Tom of the last letter and evidently working for the same company, has not yet heard from the president concerning the workers pay. The "president" is most likely the president of the mining company Marks and Tom were working for. Many of the smaller mining companies did not know one month to the next if they would make payroll.

Marks, it appears, is now suffering from their financial insecurity, as were many men.

Marks often refers to Rosa as his "pet," his "little girl," his "baby." Such expressions give the impression that Rosa was someone he considered needed to be taken care of, that Marks was her protector. From other letters, it seems the opposite case, Rosa being the stronger one looking out for Marks.

Donnie, the woman Tom and Jack fought over, was a prostitute. Jack, maybe the man who was involved with Rosa.

Charles Boscowitz was the brother of Frank Boscowitz, 27, who ran a successful clothing store on North Carson Street in Carson City. Apparently, Boscowitz had cheated Rosa out of money, a frequent occurrence.

Dora was a prostitute and Peter, her pimp.

Jim Breen at this time was a miner, became a Virginia City policeman, and finally ran the U.S. Saloon in Virginia City 1887-88. His girl, Molly O'Neil, sometimes called Margaret, was a prostitute.

Ernest Marks:
Gold Hill
Dec 27, 1878

My Own Rosa,
Your promised and very loving letter I am most thankful to received this day— thank you darling. I am always so happy to hear from you. Today I am feeling fine only I am so nervous that I can hardly write. I drink so little now I suppose is the reason but I feel better for it and I look ever so much better.

I was in Virginia last night till 10 oclock when I was coming home I met Dan. "Halow! Dan! I said. How are you Deacon, he said. I went on. But he turned, I say! I was redy for I expected trouble. I turned, well I said: Where is Rosa he said—In Carson I have been told, I said. Yes, I heard she was there he says, but she will starve there. I don't know I am certain, I said, but I hope not. "She went out of town broke," he says. Yes, I remarked, I was told the same thing. I had a row with her but I tried to make it right by offering her $40— but she was to stubborn she did not get a cent. I should have given her a $100 if she had taken the $40 by God I was going to do it, no mistake but she put it on a little too thick, but she is the best little woman I ever met no mistake and it was not her fault, it was that s of a b Mollie O'Neil— the dirty b— just let me meet her g-d her, for if I don't fix her— He had plenty of opportunitys I guess but I did not say so. I came very near telling him if he thought so much of you, he might send you some money now but thought I had better not. He says Mollie O'Neil is in Carson to. It was all news to me so I led him to believe and I don't care weather he believes it or not. I think he is drinking— he looks that way and acts kind of stupid. I guess he feels it I hope he may the brute. Yes, as you say, God speed all travelers. I may see him in Bode [Bodie?] as I have an

91

application for a situation out there. What my prospects are I don't know yet. My watching job has petered out. I have a $100 coming. I shall soon be among the mash [unemployed.]

I have a new suit making. I shall go up to try on the coat this evening, a new hat, a pair of $12 shoes. I shall be looking creditable to my Rosa when I come down. What do you say?

Your bird is singing so pretty today. You will be surprised when you see him you will think its Erni alive again.

I suppose you leave yourself out to count Em in among the six beauties—Well love you are handsomer in my eyes than any one I know.

It is very cold here now at night. I shall tell Oily Gammon what you said—he sends his regards to you. I suppose you have seen Reynolds by this time. Gammon is very attentive to his Donnie.he is there every evening now he tells me— he is as badly stuck as I am after my darling. But God ain't he jealous, the old fool— She calls him Papa.

I got a wall pocket for Christmas. I am glad you were pleased with my presents to you. I am glad to here Miss Jennie and Em liked you so well as to give you a present, but they don't think one half as much as I do my baby. I shall be down soon I hope but I don't know where Ormsby Street is—so you must tell me as near as you can— and which way the numbers run so that I may find you if I come— if I come I say— but you bet I will come if I am not dead before I am redy. I shall bring you the bird to. You might meet me if it not to far and the weather permitin. I suspect it will snow soon again—

My gov is down sick again. His old chum rheumatism is with him—and he has got the Gov on his back but it is not bad however— Christmas whiskey is the cause I guess— he was well till Ed gave him some money. That did the business-

Peacock still lives and is as fat as ever —Ed sent for his girl from your town yesterday and I guess they are angry at one another— She is to much of a flirt, Ed should not complain as he got in his work and it cost him very little— He and his red headed girl are all ok again— so I am told. I guess I am the virtuous one of all the boys now— Oily Gammon says it will be like a new married couple when you and Rosa meet again—When do you go, he said. I told him I did not know. He got his girl some presents. I will tell you about it when I see you— don't you hope it will be soon, I do—I also have a good joke to tell you on Bob when I see you, he told me of it yesterday—I had a good laugh

at him I have no more to write so I shall be off to town—
Love and Kiss for my own darling—as ever Your loving and
affectionate Erni

A week since his last letter, Marks is in better spirits though he is soon to be unemployed. He is on the wagon now. His nervousness is evidence of his severe alcohol problem. Rosa, as you will see, encouraged Marks to not drink. This may have been for his own good, or to keep him away from other prostitutes.

Marks' description of his meeting with Dan reveals more about Rosa. She has left Virginia City broke. Another customer has failed to pay up. Dan owes Rosa $140 but offers her $40. Her pride offended, Rosa explodes and gives Dan a good verbal licking which earns Dan's respect.

But Marks does not defend Rosa. He knows nothing of her affairs. Marks wants to keep his relationship with Rosa secret. He is sensitive to criticism as an analysis of his handwriting proves.

"I suppose you leave yourself out to count Em [Emma] among the six beauties." Rosa is working at Jennie Moore's house in Carson City with six other girls. Rosa does not consider herself pretty though we know from her photo she was very attractive. This is the first hint of Rosa's lack of self-esteem.

Tom Reynolds, a Gold Hill hides and pelt dealer and frequent customer, has been to Carson for his weekly visit to Rosa.

Oily Gammon, an older man and friend of Marks', is now devoting his nights to Donnie, the prostitute Tom and Jack nearly fought over.

Rosa has only recently moved to Carson. Marks has not visited her there yet and does not know where Ormsby Street is, the red light district. He asks Rosa for directions. He will bring her pet bird.

The "gov" is Marks' father, who has rheumatism and an alcohol problem.

Ed, Marks' good friend, is seeing red headed Mable Grey, a notorious prostitute. Marks still feigning his virtue to Rosa.

Gold Hill, Nevada
Dec. 30. 1878

My Darling,
 Many thanks for your loveing letter today of the 28, it was the one I expected yesterday — Yes dear I was very nervous, but I am sorry to think that you do not believe that I had not been drinking after me telling you I had not, but it is usual. No one thinks me capable of a good action. I shall take the game as well as the name, though I have entirely quit.
 The grand change has been terrible. I have been lost and not myself at all.
 Last night I was in Virginia and went down C St with two school girls. I saw Dan and he took it all in. One was in black and I guess he kind of thought it was you, but you would make two of that little dame. I guess I shall find the house without any trouble, when I come down. I guess I should have found it any how with much trouble.
 Reynolds is still here. he told Oily Gammon that he, Reynolds, would go down this week but though Reynolds has plenty of money he hates to give it up, though he appears to be pretty badly stuck after you. There is nothing new. You can expect me this week — I don't feel like writing any more now. should like to write a long letter but I am disgusted and blue everything is going wrong again today with me. I guess I shall get my money next month. Ed and Gammon are OK. I am all anxiety to see my love-by-by Love and kiss
yours always,
Erni

Written three days since his last letter, this shows how frequently Marks and Rosa wrote each other. Though recently invented, telephones were not in general use and telegrams were too expensive. Letters were the only means of communication for the lovers some fifteen miles apart.

Though Marks has claimed in several letters that he is being good and staying on the wagon, Rosa, an intelligent girl, knows Marks all too well. Soon as pressures mount, Marks will be drinking.

Marks himself claims that, "no one thinks me capable of

a "good action." His failures weighed heavily upon him. One feels he is struggling to do more with his life, but his failures drive him back to drink. His poor self-image sticks with him, a shadow he cannot shake. He is soon to visit his girlfriend at a Carson City whorehouse.

The following letter is from a Mrs. Carr, written after the recent news of her daughter's death.

New York
Jan, 4, 1879

Miss Rosa May
My dear Friend-
I was sorry to hear of my poor childs death and thank you very kindly for answering my letter. I am very glad her body was not opened but I would like to know the cause of her death-
I thank you and the other ladies for the kind interest you have taken in my daughter and God bless you all for your kindness.
I did not receive your letter till yesterday and it was a sad blow to me. I feel heart broken— I am very glad to know there is going to be a stone on her grave. If I only had the means I would love to go on and see her body now but I haven't the means to do so.
You said if you could get any further information you would let me know. I shall be very thankful to hear anything that concerns my poor daughter or anything that belonged to her and may God reward you for all your kindness to me. If there is any thing there belonging to her that would be valuable to me as keepsakes if you could send them on I would be grateful. Direct a letter to
Mrs.Carr
180 West 10th Street, New York
If you would send me the address of the woman with whom she boarded I could write her and find out the particulars about her sickness. It is very singular what ailed her. I would like to know what caused her death.
I thank you again for your kindness and close
your grateful friend
Mrs. Carr
My daughter's name was Mamie Nenninger

Mrs. Carr's thankful letter is one of several indications that Rosa May was thoughtful and kind hearted.

Some time in December, 1878, a friend of Rosa's died. She was a prostitute and may have died from one of the many venereal diseases.

Rosa's kind letter to Mrs. Carr, brought good news to the grieving mother that Rosa and other prostitutes had pitched in and bought her daughter a grave stone. Rosa did not know the dead girl's real name, and was forced to ask her mother. Most prostitutes went under assumed names. We do not know whether Mrs. Carr knew that her daughter, Mamie Nenninger, was a prostitute.

Mrs. Carr's letter was addressed to Rosa May at 18 South D Street, Cad Thompson's brothel. Rosa must have gone back to Virginia City from Carson when she learned of Mamie's death. This leads one to assume that Mamie died in Virginia City. However, a search of death records in the Virginia City courthouse showed no record of death for any woman in December, 1878.

I spent several hours under a broiling August sun searching the Virginia City cemeteries for Mamie Nenninger's grave, but could not find it.

Another letter from Ernest Marks, addressed to Rosa in Carson City:

At Home [Gold Hill]
Sunday Jany 5, 1879

Rosa Darling,
Now I shall answer your loveing letter of the 2nd inst. Yes, I thought the card rather neat and it was so [Indecipherable] *...during the day and you were pleased.*

Yes love I am a good boy and shall try to be. No! Pet I did-not get into some girls box, but Tom did-Donnie gave him that paper and I wrote that letter in his room and he gave me that paper. Oh! no! my Rosa, rather say that I am a convenient article for Uncle Tom. [He may mean Tom Reynolds] *Oh! no I can't have it that way for I do not want you to think that I am giving you traffic* [business] *so I don't wish you to say you suppose it is all right, when I know baby mine that though you say it is all right, you feel in your dam good heart that you mean it is all wrong. No! No! Rosa, if I should do anything wrong Oily Gammon would only be the first to tell it to someone so that you could hear it.*

I have not got my new suit yet. The taylors all got drunk so I was disappointed in not getting it as soon as I expected it. But I hope to get them this week and then darling if my new job has given out please look out for your baby. My new business keeps me busy—but I guess it will not last much longer. I can't say that I am stuck after it but it will get a few dollars.

New Years I had my black suit on and I looked so, I was often told during the day, real sweet and nice. I got on very nice did not get tight. Three drinks was all I took during the day and I felt good the next morning. Last night I took in Vovoneys Sorrie and had rather a pleasant time.

I guess you have seen the long expected Reynolds by this time as he left here the other day to go to Reno and I heard him say that he was going to stay in Carson two days and then agoing to San Francisco.

Ed has his red headed darling down here at some rooms up town. [Red heads were considered best in bed.] *She came down last night and stayed with him and is still there and will go back tonight. She is rather pleasant. I met her today when I returned from the p.o.* [post office] *I was disappointed in not getting a letter from you today- ByBy darling bless my baby Sweet Kisses Write soon your loving Erni*

It is difficult to discern what moral code, if any, that Rosa and Marks lived by. We know that Rosa has accused Marks of getting in some girls "box." Rosa does not want Marks sleeping with other women. Nor does she like the idea of him sending her "traffic," business.

Evidently, Rosa has told Marks, "If it's all right for you to send me your friends, it's all right for me to take their money." She seems to be testing Mark's love. Marks plays along. "I don't wish you to suppose it is all right, when I know baby mine that you mean it is all wrong."

Marks is still living in Gold Hill and has a new job. We

do not know what kind of work it is.

As always, Marks is defensive about his drinking, claiming he's only had three drinks New Year's Day. Unlike other lovers, Marks and Rosa did not spend Christmas nor New Year's together.

Tom Reynolds has made his visit to Rosa.

Ed and Mable Grey are together again. Ed keeping Mable in rooms away from his and Marks' place.

The following letter from Marks was addressed to Rosa at No. 1 Ormsby Street, Carson City:

January 7, 1879
Gold Hill

Oh You Darling,
You don't know how glad I was this evening to hear from you. I was very much disappointed in not getting a letter from you yesterday but I suppose you're never too busy to write.

My love, your letter sounds as though you feel hurt. It is so unlike you. I'm sorry to see you feeling as you do and I think it is unkind of you to feel that way towards me for though you may think because I do not answer your letters as promptly as usual that I'm off on something else. I can tell you darling that there is nothing in it and I do hope darling one you will believe to be of old your Ernest and no one else's for I have not since you have gone had anything to do with woman or single girl or married, widow or grass widow [a woman divorced or separated from her husband] *or woman of any kind. This may seem strange to you who knows me so well but it is the truth as sure as I write this. The doctor* [his penis] *seems to think of no one else but his Rosa's doctoress* [you can guess]. *And as for taking interest or pleasure in my new job, I cannot see where the pleasure comes to wrangle all day with creditors and their bills. I thought my job would end last week. I was to be paid ten dollars for writing up a small set of books that they thought would take me two days. I did it in only one and then they wanted me to stay and take in the money and I am still at it for you know what few dollars I get I very much need.*

I might have come down to see you Sunday but I should have had to be back Sunday night. What good would that have been? I thought more so I stayed at home but now have an idea of coming down Saturday night with the horse and back Monday. If I do I will let you know before I come if you say that I may come.

 Reynolds was in your house last night but you were engaged and he left. He went to San Francisco tonight. He told Oily Gammons that the house was doing a land office business and he did not want to get a wet dick.

 I am sorry that I was not on the train Friday to meet my love but I hope you will think no harm in it and not feel hard toward your baby for I meant not to fool you and would not willingly disappoint my pet for any consideration. Why Rosa do you say good-bye, no more love and kisses for me and you wish to be [indecipherable] *sometimes.*

  For today there is no hard task
  No burden that I would not bear with grace
  No sacrifice I could name or ask
  That were granted could I see your sweet face

 Oh Rosa how can you think for a moment that good-bye. Remember we sometimes should not [indecipherable] *felt by me. Pet I do not write to you in any such strain but my love I know you do not mean it Millions of kisses and lodes of love -*
Ernest

The pimp or boyfriend was the most important person in a prostitute's superficial life. He was someone she could talk to about her work; someone who gave her attention. Rosa May chose Ernest Marks to be that person, although he was unstable, often drunk, untrustworthy and unable to give of himself emotionally.

Marks and Rosa are quarreling. She has scolded him for not writing promptly. Rosa is hurt and feels that Ernest has made a fool of her by not coming down to Carson the previous Friday when he was expected. She is worried his new job is taking him away from her. And, she fears that Marks is sleeping with other women, the supreme rejection.

By not visiting her, not writing and sleeping with other women, Rosa feels uneasy about their relationship. Fearing Ernest will soon reject her, Rosa breaks off with Ernest. But Marks plays innocent. It is unlike her to be hurt, he says. He has not slept with anyone. His job is of no great importance and he will come down Saturday and stay till Monday. He pleads with her, writes four lines of poetry and asks her forgiveness. He does not seem to fear that her anger will last. He knows Rosa.

Reynolds was down to see Rosa Saturday night. The brothel was busy.

February 5, 1879
Gold Hill

Darling Rosa,

your long expected letter is here at last. I am so glad I should not have had time to answer it today but I was down here to see some parties against whom I had some bills. You don't know how glad I am to receive your letter. It is very short but I suppose there is no scandal in you being busy. I'm glad to hear that times are getting better with you and I hope that they will keep on improving with my baby.

I should judge from reading your letter that you had a drinking party at your house. [Indecipherable] *I wrote you yesterday which note I suppose you have today, I began to feel anxious thinking that your prospects* [indecipherable] *had happened. I came very near to passing in my chips the other night but today I'm all o.k. except that my neck is just a little stiff and my head and* [indecipherable].

If this beautiful weather keeps on I must try and get down and see you Sunday. I took in Ed's shooting gun and got some rabbits [indecipherable] *has been sick only Gammon and I have been able to see. Also he and that dame have been living in town together I believe. Ed still has got his red headed girl. She is going to move into Molly Ashton's today and there will be three or four more for the boys today. Ed says that his baby tells him that Weston pays his girls to sell wine for him. Ed I guess is trying to get me away from my pet I suppose he thinks I need a little but I don't unless I get it from my baby.*
Love and kisses for my dearest Rosa.
Emi

It has been a month since Marks' last letter. He is a bill

collector. Rosa's letter is short. Marks doesn't mind nor does he mind that business is picking up for Rosa. She is having more men and earning more money. "I'm glad to hear that times are getting better with you..."

Marks' friend, Oily Gammon and his girl, Donnie are living together. Mable Grey, the infamous, is still with Ed. Mable will soon be working at Molly Ashton's brothel, along with three or four new girls.

Weston, a brothel owner, pays his girls to hustle wine, a common custom. Marks still feigning his virtue.

February 11, 1879
Gold Hill

My Own Darling,

Thanks to you and the railroad here I am again. I had six minutes to spare when I got to the train. I'm not feeling very bright today my head is hurting me again. I saw Oily and his girl today. They are fine it seems. Ed was sorry he returned home but thought it was better because his strawberry blonde might find it out.

It looks like a storm here today, the wind is blowing pretty hard. The wind Saturday night in Virginia [indecipherable] *It did not storm here like it did in your town.*

McGrath was caught in bed with Mrs. Noel Crowell, a dressmaker and milkman on C Street and got kicked out by her husband. He is ole Beecher and I have known him for a long time. Man is frail and only a man but Mrs. Noel Crowell. Oh, such taste but they are something of [indecipherable] *but only for their bad looks and she more than he for her gin pressing habits. That little red headed dame came up at the train. I guess she belongs at the* [indecipherable]

My Dad is feeling better and is now getting about the house a little and managed to get a clean shave yesterday so he is looking pretty well. I hope you are over your fright I guess it is all o.k.

The doctor seems himself but it is not time for him but I am not at all uneasy about him. He is such a [indecipherable] *I am not about to* [indecipherable] *love and kisses, Erni*

Marks has been down to visit Rosa in Carson City. She

has paid his train fare back to Gold Hill. They have been drinking. Marks is hung over.

Oily and Donnie are fine but Ed's sneaking around on Mable. Marks referring to his penis, "I am not at all uneasy about him," probably means that he has not caught disease from Rosa.

February 15, 1879
Gold Hill

My love,
your dear kind and loving letter I am in receipt of today. Thank you darling for being so prompt in answering my letters. Yes I did ride [possibly write] to San Francisco to get a place but not for me but for a friend who in former days was superintendent of mines here. I wrote to him to see if he could get me a place somewhere. I did not ask him to get it in any particular camp or place only so I got a situation. God forgive me Rosa, its breaking my heart to sit here doing nothing and you in that damn town. I want to take you out of it or help you along.

I am told that Reynolds was engaged to that young lady in Empire but it is all moon knocked in the head and that they are seven. It was by some married woman in Virginia and he has also got himself into another scrape so I was told.

There is a married woman in Virginia Oily Gammons, Johny Hobart, John Strammon, Henry Gusten and Reynolds have got to. Reynolds was the last of all. She's now 4 months in the family way and she says it was Tom Reynolds who done it. Anyway she said she will make him pay for it so Gammons says.

No Oily has not got that money. I was told in Virginia that it would be here in a few days to pay all hands. And yes you are right dear, he is Oily Gammons, but he better not ever do anything of that kind. Stone cutting at Carson has no charms for Oily Gammons. It is an old saying, love is blind but darling it is not in this case of ours.

Many thanks for your pretty and appropriate Valentine. No post mark on it but I know it is from you. Mother is going to give me a frame to put it in. I send you one. I saw some pretty ones but my bank account has gone where the woodbine twineth.

I guess Ed and his dame will soon quit. He's getting his eyes opened. You are right, they do not love as we do. In fact she is only a money getting creature and that is all she thinks of. I can't say I like her at all. She has too much deceit in her to suit me. She is not like my baby. Oh you darling.

> *For this belief whatever betide*
> *Though friends prove false and court each eye*
> *At morn and noon when night's set free*
> *I'll fondly love, bless and think of thee Rose*

I give all my love and kisses to my darling.
Always thine baby.
Ernest

Marks is out of work, unable to send Rosa a Valentine's card. He is living with his father and mother. He has written someone in San Francisco seeking a job for an old friend, a former mine superintendent. A superintendent was a position of great responsibility and good pay. He oversaw the workings of the entire mine often deciding which direction a drift or stope should be run.

Marks is seeking work elsewhere as the economic depression deepens along the Comstock and more men are laid off.

Ernest does seem to be genuinely concerned for Rosa when he says, "God forgive me Rosa, its breaking my heart to sit here doing nothing and you in that damn town. I want to take you out of it or help you along."

That "damn town," of course, was Carson City, a jumping off place for travelers heading south to the recent boom camp of Bodie, or north to Reno and San Francisco. Many were leaving Virginia City for Bodie. Each day stages left Carson full of passengers. They were followed by twenty horse teams hauling great mining equipment to the boom camp. With so many travelers passing through town, Carson City was more profitable for Rosa than Virginia City.

Carson City was then a town of five to seven thousand. Many were employed by the Carson and Tahoe Lumber Company, located a mile south of the red light district. Its great yard was a mile long and half a mile wide. A twelve mile flume from Spooner's Summit in the Sierra above Lake Tahoe, carried the newly cut timber down from the mountains to Carson. The wood

103

was used in the Virginia City and Gold Hill mines which had already consumed millions of board feet. Cities of timbers lay beneath these two camps.

The Carson City Mint, several blocks from the red light district, employed many men. Others found work in Empire City, a suburb in east Carson along the Carson River where stamp and saw mills were located. And of course there were travelers. From these men Rosa May and other prostitutes earned their livings.

It appears that Marks' family lived in Gold Hill. He has mentioned his father, a sister and now his mother. He also had a brother, Morris, who opened a wholesale liquor business in Bodie in 1880. Ernest later worked for him.

From this letter it seems that Rosa and Ernest were able to love one another in some peculiar way. They had something. They were together off and on for thirty-five years.

Gold Hill
1879

My Dear Rosa,
What is the matter? You are not sick I hope. I am feeling anxious about you as I should surely. Haven't a letter from you today or yesterday. But I don't know what's the matter with my pet. I am unable to work anymore, I am sick. I took a fall which has laid me up today but I am up again. My neck and head feel funny. Reynolds to Em kindness and best wishes. Good luck and lots of luck I am always yours. Love and kisses. Erni.

April 17, 1879
Gold Hill

Dear Rosa,
you dear loving girl, your letter is here all o.k and have perused it. I must say that I was correct in calling you a bad guesser for I had put it up that you were only guessing. As I said before there is nothing in it. I don't let them bother me at all.
I see by this morning's paper that Alex Crane and Dora Elliot

got married on the 15th in Virginia. Good enough. And that Robert Hill Lindsay has got to Annie Baugerman by marrying her at the residence of her poppa and mamma and it goes as it layest. I hope it may be a success. Bob has worked at that thing a good long time now but I can't say I admire his taste at all. She's rather smart and pleasant but homely but then its nice to have a little. I can't say she has any unless its below her chin.

Tonight, tomorrow night and the next night we shall have the Bergois in the opera house. As usual, I don't go, I have seen them before 2 or 3 times, that is enough.

Ed received yesterday three pictures of his Mabel all in different positions and they look well. I must say she appears to be in very good health. He is very much tickled over them. I made a [indecipherable] *The five pictures are different. Just think of it.*

Peter Saltry [possibly Faltry or Daltry] *as well as Bell Saltry has got the grand bounce. It seems it was Miss Peel that homely that he thought himself so solid with, in fact all the losers got the grand.*

Peel has got herself another fellow, by the name of Terry a soft fool. Peter and Bell Saltry would have had a fight night before last if it had not been for [undecipherable] *Both made it up we don't care. Saltry's are N.G. and don't forget it.*

I send you the china. [money] *You just bet I am a good boy and all my love and kisses belong to Rosa. Regards to Em. I am always your wild dutchman.   Ernie*

Rosa may have told Marks in her last letter, that she feels Ernest is troubled by the opinions of others regarding their relationship. But Ernest defends himself, "I don't let them bother me," which could not have been true. Marks was sensitive to criticism. Rosa here, using her fine intuition.

Alex Crane was an assistant foreman at the Ophir Mine, 1873-74. It was a position of good pay and responsibility. In 1875 he was a teamster and lived on South D Street near the red light district. In 1883-84 he was a shaftman for the C and C and lived in a lodging house at 8 North C Street.

Robert Hill Lindsay, Jr., was the son of Robert Hill Lindsay, City Attorney for Virginia City, and one of the original forty-niners.

Mabel has sent Ed nude pictures of herself. Peter and Bell Saltry, low-lifes, were run out of town.

April 22, 1879
Gold Hill

Rosa Darling,
your dear kind and loving letter I received yesterday. I know my pet that you are disappointed this morning that I did not answer it as soon as I received it. But I was to have something to do yesterday by making an appearance in Virginia. I was there nearly all day but as my usual luck I did not get it. So baby of mine I hope you will excuse my not having written you.

I did not see those dizzy dames from your city. I guess China Charlie knows what he is talking about when he says the girls are making nothing. It is fearful dull and the boys are in the same boat as the girls. They don't appear to have a cent or are hardly making anything.

Cino is working for Tom Duncan and Joe Gavin. He appears to be very steady. I never see him with a cut mouth at all. He appears to be having a good close game of it now and I like many others, are glad of it. The certainty [?] bis has not started yet. Benster, Joe, George Green and some others besides Petro are not going to work it. I don't know how it will go as there is a law against it in this state.

Matt Canavan's underground party was a grand thing about 100 people attended. Ed took a girl. He and Brad drank wine out of goblets. There was plenty of it and I was told it was rather a jolly crowd after supper. They danced till 4 o'clock Sunday morning. I don't think Mrs. Canavan went to church as usual that morning, Cutt Mouth [indecipherable] nor Jim Sheridan went there. Pete Dunn and more of the gang were there however.

Weather is fine today but Saturday night and Sunday, fearful cold and windy. There don't seem to be as many people in town as usual.I [indecipherable]. I hear Weston is going to have some new girls soon and Cad Thompson also.I don't see why, there appears to be too many now.

I'm sorry to hear my baby that you are falling back but you are in better luck than most of them it seems.

Jack Brady was asking about you yesterday. I told him you were fine the last time I saw you, about a month ago. It is getting to be a long time my girl. I keep trying to make a piece but it seems I can't. Forever like you dear self, I live in hopes of better times.

I had quite a talk with Dan the other day. I started it but he never mentioned your name. He was on horse back going to Gold Hill he said.With my best wishes. I am only yours. Regards to Emma. Erni

Hard times on the Comstock. There are too many prostitutes in Virginia City and they are not making enough. The men as the women do not have much money. Rosa is earning less and complains of it.

Throughout this period, Virginia City's *Territorial Enterprise*, noted increased brawling in saloons. Many were arrested for drunk and disorderly conduct, the highest crime in the camp. Out of work and frustrated, men became violent.

Tom Duncan, 37, was a gambler. Whatever Benster, Joe Gavin, George Green and Petro are doing, it is illegal. Crime increased with the bad times.

Matt Canavan was a superintendent of the New York mine in Gold Hill, a lesser mine. Jim Sheridan was a miner. Pete Dunn, an Irishman, was a bartender in 1875, had his own saloon in 1880-81 and was Storey County Assessor 1883-84.

Weston ran a brothe1. He and Cad Thompson are bringing in new girls.

Jack Brady may be the Jack of an earlier letter. Checking his name, there were two in Virginia City, one a miner; the other a teamster.

Gold Hill
June 3, 1879

Dear Rosa,
Your very welcome letter came to hand yesterday evening. I was so glad to see that it was your old self who wrote it. I am real glad to know that you are enjoying the boss blessing—good health.I wish I could say as much. I feel as though I was in the family way and look thin and care worn. I don't know why it should be but it is.

I feel happy and why shouldn't I,I have such a darling good girl. I will soon be done with my job. It will not turn out as good as I expected. Still, I will get something out of it. It has been a hard job, and raised some blisters I can tell you.

It is very warm here now and such pretty nights. Last night the moon appeared to have a black eye as in [indecipherable]

From your letter, Dutch Kate must have good booze again,as she or rather her husband.

Scotty as usually cared not to keep away from the faro games and it went where the woodbine twineth.

Sister Eva is keeping house for Inez I am told. Mable is the only girl in the house who is making room, rent and grub. Oh George, this cousin of yours [indecipherable] *often mentions one friend* [indecipherable] *She the grand dame with so many ladies, likes quality, is a beautiful strawberry blonde and to the bargain.*

Ed says Daisy, [indecipherable]*, Fanny went with some minstrel to Carson on a drunk and I was told that Miss Rouse returned with some new stock also that Tom Simfawcett is now the boss with Inez. Must be a good one or good for nothing, we don't care. Ed and a friend are going to Steamboat* [hot springs] *next week. Oily Gammons has started his mine up, put on his brother in law, as watchman, in fact he is the only man at it in and about the mine. I guess it will not be as good as it seemed. So as the rough and ready. Regards to Em.*[Emma]

Love and kisses to my pet. Erni

Nearly two months since Marks's last letter. Difficult to say whether letters written in between this time were lost over the years.

Rosa has recovered from another illness; we do not know what it was.

Dutch Kate was a Carson City madam. Inez ran a brothel in Virginia City. Mabel is now one of her girls, a boarder, and the "only girl making room rent and grub."

Often, girls in a large house were called, "boarders" because they rented a room from the madam. After paying rent, whatever a girl made was hers. This differed from madams who ran houses on percentage basis, where a girl received only so much for a "trick." Evidently, Inez was using the boarder method. In efforts to replenish business, madams often changed girls. Popular girls who made good money, were kept on. Those who didn't were shown the door.

Prostitutes were entertainers of a sort and moved from brothel to brothel. Even among prostitutes, there was status. Parlor house girls had the number one position. They were most often the prettiest. They were fed and clothed by the madam and saw the more affluent customers.

Below this was the crib girl, who rented a small two room building. After paying rent, whatever the crib girl made was hers.

There were, of course, common street hookers who searched the streets for customers. Compared to the parlor house girl, who was protected and had the camaraderie of other girls, the street hooker had it tough. She was open to the worst abuse, theft, beatings and murder. A street hooker became hardened in little time.

Perhaps worst, were the "cow yards." In San Francisco's Barbary Coast, a run down, cut-throat district, these were run-down hotels filled with fifty to a hundred tired prostitutes. Here girls made 25 or 30 cents a trick.

Rosa May was twenty-four in 1879, still pretty enough to be kept on in the Carson and Virginia City whorehouses.

Miss Rouse was another Virginia City madam, who has recently brought in new "stock."

Tom Simfawcett is now Inez's pimp and lover.

Steamboat Springs is a hot spring resort in Pleasant Valley on U.S. 395 between Carson City and Reno. Its waters are as hot as they were in Rosa's time. Some buildings date back to the 1870's.

By this letter, we see Marks was quite familiar with Comstock's various brothels, madams, girls and pimps. So were many men living on the Comstock. Marks took particular interest in their doings, due to his desires, and for Rosa's sake, who may have needed a place in one of the houses.

June 11, 1879
Gold Hill

Dear Rosa,
when I arrived yesterday I went down to see how my man was getting

on which was very slow I must say. I worked a while there, came home and fell asleep. I feel very mean today. It is raining and I feel like an iceberg. Ed looked very cross when I got back. I suppose Miss Mabel had to attend to someone else's business as usual not her own but it made no difference for he said nothing. He told Oily Gammons I was a hell of a fellow, which I guess is true enough. I don't know if he will be off on his trip tomorrow or not.I hope he may for I should like to see him away for awhile, away for a few days so he may look more pleasant than he has for some time. That red headed dame is leading him a sorry life of it I think, for he is not of yore. But it is not my business for I wouldn't make an example to anyone. He was looking well. I cannot write anymore. I feel miserable. Ed and Bob took over the fish.
love and kisses, Ernie
P.S. I forgot to say that I missed you in the morning, thanks for the same.

Marks has been to Carson to see Rosa. He was up most of the night drinking. He's tired and hung over.

Mabel Grey, the red head, a troublesome woman is leading Ed a sorry life. Ed is as depressed as Marks.

June 12, 1879
Gold Hill

Dear Rosa,
I'm happy to acknowledge the safe arrival of your dear kind letter today. Ed, as I said before nothing to you, I judge that Mabel told him about me. From his looks, I guess he and her will soon quit for it is now busted and I was told it was not him but some other fellow who was going to keep her. He was away with a cat last night, one of those Sunday school kind who cheat the regular out of what belongs to them. He is as true and constant to his Mabel as the wind and weather in this country.

I saw George Green and he wanted to know where he knew you. I told him I did not know. He was somewhat bothered about your telling about Viola and Weston being at the picnic. I laughed but never let on that I knew any thing about it.

Saltry got drunk Monday night and fell down the stairs in one of the houses of joy and has got one of his eyes in mourning to look at in the glass as he stands behind the bar.

I see by the paper this morning that Johnny Hobart is gone to Australia and it reads to me as if Johnny is not the only one in the family that was on it. I may misunderstand it but I would not blame her if she did Hobart [indecipherable], no reason for his departure and she returned to her home in San Francisco. Perhaps she was down there on a visit and he was an unexpected arrival. Be that how it may I don't care for I know how it is myself but I was never like him myself.

I got my job done and now the [indecipherable] but there is little left in it.

The doctor, I'm happy to let you know, is well and quite as of yore.

I did not think you cared to get that house for certain. "Our Luck" as usual. Don't you know I'm getting tired of such luck. I'm getting to be a chronic grouch.

Weather beautiful today, very little rain. Regards to Em [Emma] respectfully yours, Erni

Marks has fooled around with Mabel, Ed's red head. Ed and Mabel are soon to part and another man will keep her.

Don't know who George Green, Viola nor Johnny Hobart were. Weston, Virginia City brothel owner, mentioned again.

Saltry, who in an earlier letter was bounced from town, has fallen down stairs in a Virginia brothel.

Rosa had evidently wanted to rent a certain house in Virginia City. She and Marks have missed their opportunity. Marks complains here, and in other letters about their bad luck.

June 14, 1879
Gold Hill

Dear Rosa,
your dear letter found today as usual. I am very glad to hear that you are enjoying yourself so nicely. If this is a short and poorly written letter please excuse me for I am in a very poor humor. My damn bad luck follows everyone as well as I. Yesterday as they were milling my stuff, there was a rock in it and it broke a pan and caused a loss of $200

to my friend who was working it for me. Damn such luck I say. I expected to get it returned today but now won't until next week.

Ed goes to Tahoe tomorrow by Carson and Glenbrook to Hot Springs. He will not stay long and I shall run the business while he's gone. God and the devil will keep my good luck right with you while Ed is away. I can't stand it but the best thing to do I suppose is to endure it. But that is getting very monotonous. I know. I have not drunk a drop since last I saw you and the boys don't know what to make of it. Oily Gammons looks at me as if I was off my nut and I guess [indecipherable] Oily and his dame got thrown out of a buggy the other day but did not get hurt, has a wagon and a blacksmith bill to pay however. I guess he will pay it if money comes.

There was 27 car loads that went to the picnic this morning, principally tid bits and tid bit hunters. I expect they will have a good time. I might have went but my last picnic was enough. I expect next month will be a grand picnic for me, it is hard to tell yet. I send you the china. [money]

Bill and Fred make a fine team. I wonder where they got their money, from someone else I guess. Be good. Regards to Emma. Good luck. all my love, Erni

Marks seems to be involved in mining now. He has obtained some ore and a friend is milling it.

To mill ore, it must first be pulverized. It is then mixed with water and various chemicals in a large round pan which spins at high speed. The pan is much like a kitchen mixer and does just about the same job. Mercury is added, causing the silver to amalgamate.

It seems, while Marks' ore was being milled, a rock caused one of the pans to break, a freak accident. This has caused he and his friend to lose $200.

Ed and Marks are running some kind of business, it may have been a saloon. Marks would later run a saloon in Bodie.

One of the most popular summer pastimes for people living in Virginia City, were the picnics at Farmer Treadway's in Carson City. Treadway owned a large park with many trees, lush grass and a dance hall. The greenery was a welcome sight for Virginia City people as there was little of it in that mining camp.

On these picnics, there were special trains at cut prices which took carloads of people down to Carson. On this one particular picnic, Marks says there were 27 carloads.

July 30, 1879
Gold Hill

Dear Rosa,
your very short and cross letter is at hand today. I suppose you should write me in that strain. My neglect of you, or more properly speaking, your letters, was not caused by an attention to anybody else or by putting my time against anyone else but by business I was attending to for Ed. But as he returned I am once again able to answer your letters as before. It seems strange to me that you of all others should write as you do but I suppose you believe what you write, therefore you do so because you think it is true and right that you should do so.

I'm very sorry that I cannot do as you requested. But the china [money] and another small package was in the post office before I read your letter so I hope you will overlook it if it is wrong. It seems so strange that my bad luck should come between you and I. It makes me feel bad that you would believe that I don't think of you as I always did. You can think as you please for it is a privilege we all have and I shall do the same, I shall not quarrel.

> *0 pardon the crowds awhile*
> *I waste one thought I owe to thee*
> *And self-condemned appear to smile*
> *Unfaithful to thy memory*
> *Nor deem that memory less dear*
> *That then I seem not to repine*
> *I would not fools should hear*
> *One sigh that I should wholly be thine*

I have got 2 blisters and it is doing me no good to write as I do. I am very, very hurt to see you wrote good-bye. I hope you don't mean it. I said nothing to you when you went to the dinner party and did not write me for days. I don't suppose all my writing will mend the matter or get me forgiven. My regards to Em. Love and kisses to yourself and believe as everyone

Erni

Rosa is again hurt because Ernest has not written her soon enough. She feels someone else is receiving his attention. In an effort to make him react in some way, she writes and breaks off with him. The ploy works. Ernest quickly writes back and attempts to reassure Rosa that he does care for her.

Marks again blames his troubles on his bad luck. The lines of poetry are his.

August 12, 1879, Rosa May returned to Virginia City. She was back at Cad Thompson's at 18 South D Street. The following letter was written by Rosa's friend, Emma, a Carson City prostitute.

Carson
August 15, 1879

Little friend Rosa,
Your letter was received yesterday. I was very glad to hear from you. I am pleased to hear that you are doing well. It must be an agreeable change to go out at night and come in the morning with a shining $20 more than you would see here in monthy. [I believe she means, "in a month."] *I am sure your room looks very nice a splendid place for your dear little Johnny* [customer] *to slip in when he comes to see you. The dreamy waltz for instance. Phil has stopped cooking and Lilly and myself eat at the restaurant and have a pretty good time. I have not drawn a sober breath since I have been home. I also received from San Jose* [a letter] *When I saw the post mark it kind of sobered me. I thought it was from home but it was from some fellow by the name of Spencer. Leilly* [Lilly] *and Wilson was at the train to meet me and I saw your dear Johnny, my Billy and Mr-Brooks was here to see me Tuesday night, but did not stay. They asked after you and told me to send their love to you when I wrote. Lilly was telling me that Mrs. Phillips said if you condescended to bid her good by she would have opened a bottle of wine, ho, ho. Tell Miss Cad Thompson that I went to see about her stockings. They did not have any at present but they sent for them and they wil be here as soon as they get them. My bird sings very sweet in the morning but not a word from him in the afternoon his voice is very weak. My Charley sends his love to you. Also Lilly and her Charley, I*

and also Emana Boyd. Give my love to Miss Cadd and remember me
kindly to all the other girls.
Answer soon.
Yours Respectfully
Emma
PS. I saw Bell Graham she sends her love to and she says we will go up
and see you soon.
Emma

This interesting and informative letter was written by Emma Hall, later, Emma Goldsmith. Emma Hall was jailed in June, 1880 in Virginia City for theft. She was 27. She was an alcoholic and eventually drank herself to death.

We do not know exactly what has caused Rosa's move back to Virginia City. She may have wanted a change, or be closer to Ernest, perhaps to make better money at Cad Thompson's. Business was bad. "Its as quiet here as ever," Emma says.

Rosa has gone out at night and made $20, a miner's week wages. One would assume that Rosa was street walking in order to implement whatever she was making at Cad Thompson's.

From this letter, it seems that Rosa was a boarder at Thompson's paying rent for a room, yet still free to work the streets. Rosa was a tidy person and took great pleasure in her surroundings. She explains to Emma that her room is looking nice, "A splendid place for your dear little Johnny." A "John," was a prostitute's customer.

Emma was from San Jose, California. She feared that the letter with the San Jose postmark was from her family. Prostitutes often feared their families would find them out.

Mr. Brooks, a customer of Emma's, was a successful Carson merchant.

Mrs. Mary Ann Phillips, then 58, was a Carson City madam for whom Rosa had most recently worked. "...if you had condescended to bid her good by," seems to imply that Rosa was very prideful and may not have left Phillips' place on the best terms.

Mining camp prostitutes were fond of birds, especially canaries. Ernest has mentioned Rosa's bird in several letters.

Emma mentions her own. The custom of mining camp prostitutes having birds, very likely came from the miner's use of canaries to detect bad air and smoke in the mines.

Emma's Charley, was Charles Young, and listed himself as, "lover," in the Virginia City 1880 Census. He was 45, and lived on South D Street. Emana Boyd was a Carson City prostitute. Rosa is one of a number of girls working at Cad Thompson's.

Virginia City
Aug. 18th 1879

Friend Leo,
Having arrived in town again I write to inform you of my address and if you wish to call and see me I would be pleased to have you do so I am living with Mrs. C. Thompson. Hoping to see you soon.
I am as ever
Yours Respectfully
Rosa May
No. 18 D St

This is the only sample of Rosa's handwriting. The note was business letter to Leo Miller, a Virginia City jeweler and a good customer.

[No date]

Miss Rosa
Please come to my room to night. If you wish come between 9 and 10. The front door will be open so walk right in to my room and I will be on up as soon as I close the store.

Isaac Isaacs.
You know where I live?

Isaac Isaacs ran a clothing store at 38 South C Street in Virginia City with a man called Cohn. Evidently, Rosa sometimes operated as a call girl. Isaacs lived at a boarding house at 31 South C Street, ran by Mrs. Leconey. The boarding house was in a brick building above McMillan's and Adams' store.

The last letter from Ernest Marks:

Happy New Year
Virginia City
January 1,1879 [he meant 1880]

My Own Rosa
  I am in receipt of both your letters. Oh! no my darling, do not
for a moment think your constant writing anoys me. God bless you if it
was not for those letters I don't know what I should do now that I have
you not in person to love, to talk to. I forgive you darling for thinking
that your dear letters disturb me. I got your powder last night at Coles
[a Virginia City drug store] *and I hope to bring it tomorrow or the*
next day. I expect it will be just my luck to meet Reynolds but I shall go
in and brave it—I am making calls. I enclose you my card and I am
wishing it might be as last year that I might present it in person. Tom
is in a great hurry stop [Indecipherable] *It is rather a nice day. I see*
many callers out. I shall write you a longer letter tomorrow. Just think
my love, I have not drank a drop today. I know you will be glad to hear
I am so good. Remember me to Em. Tom also. Oily Gammon says happy
new year to Rosa. I do to and many returns — May my darling always
be happy— Sweet Kisses lots of prosperity for 1880
Yours always
Erni

Five months since our last word, Rosa is back in Carson City. She was a faithful letter writer and fears this disturbs Marks.

Marks fears he will run into Tom Reynolds when he visits Rosa. He's on the wagon.

The next is the last letter, and an interesting one to end with. It is from Cad Thompson in San Francisco, and addressed to Rosa May at Cad Thompson's brothel in Virginia City.

San Francisco
March 27th, 1880

Friend Rosa,
  I received your letter and was glad to hear from you. I am still

crippled up with rheumatism and have not been out to see a woman Lena Beck and that Emma and Lily from Carson called to see me last nigh. Emma looks horrible and from her report of the mountains [business in Virginia City] *I guess it will be hard work to get anyone to go there. The weather has been rainy, cold, and disagreeable ever since I came down* [from Virginia City.]

Tell the Spanish woman to keep her house. I don't want it, for if there is nothing in Virginia [no business in Virginia City] *I will move my furniture down here as everyone seems to live in this place. I will try and get some women next week and run the house one trip and tell George that he need not mind whitening it until I see what we are going to do.*

I don't know why in hell Welch did not tell me what he wanted, Crittons or what he wanted and I would have sent it the same time I sent the other stuff.

I am sorry you have been sick, I don't wonder, that damp, dreary house would make any body sick, it makes me sick to think that I have got to go back to it. Give Harry's and my kind regards to George.

Hoping this finds you well and to hear from you soon. I remain yours respectfully. Mrs. C Thompson

By March 27, 1880, three months since the last letter, Rosa is again in Virginia City at Cad Thompson's brothel at 18 South D Street.

Thompson is temporarily in San Francisco with Harry, her man. She may have gone to San Francisco to give her rheumatism a rest. Virginia City's cold winters drove many rheumatoid sufferers to San Francisco.

Emma, Rosa's good friend, and Lilly are in San Francisco. Emma is looking terrible from her drinking.

I don't know who Welch or Crittons were.

Rosa has been sick again. "...I don't wonder, that damp, dreary house would make any body sick, it makes me sick to think that I have got to go back to it." Such a picture of Thompson's brothel is a far cry from the crystal chandelier, velvet curtains and flowing champagne we might otherwise imagine her place to have been. Thompson herself is not stable enough financially to stay in San Francisco. She is tied to her place in

Virginia City, though it is not doing well. "I have got to go back to it," she says.

George was probably the house bouncer and handyman.

It seems that Thompson, a stickler for details, considers Rosa one of the more responsible girls and has left her in charge of her brothel.

From this letter, one would think that Thompson would soon move to San Francisco. Times were getting harder in Virginia City for the prostitutes and madams. There was less money circulating and it was tough to get new girls to work in Virginia City. San Francisco seemed the place to be.

But Cad Thompson did not leave Virginia City in 1880. She stayed on. She was involved in two civil court matters in 1883. On June 6, 1885, the *Virginia Chronicle* carried these lines about her:

While sitting at the second-story window of her establishment on D street, last Saturday evening, the widow Thompson observed a young man whom she recognized as the 'Barbary Coast masher,' [pimp] *holding a rope behind him and trying to coax her dog away, which was sitting in the doorway. Arming herself with a large bucketful of slops, she waited until the masher grasped the dog by the collar, when she emptied the entire contents of the bucket on his person. Adonis let go his hold and lit out in the direction of the north pole, closely followed by the affronted dog and at least half a dozen fleet footed female denizens of the Thompson 'mayzong,' armed with mops and stove pokers.*

Cad Thompson, a woman of 53 in 1880, had operated brothels in Virginia City since the 1860's. She is mentioned three times *in The Journals of Alfred Doten*. Doten was owner and editor of the *Gold Hill News*, but lost the newspaper in 1878 as the Comstock declined. As a newspaperman, it was Doten's job to know the people and the doings on the Comstock. His daily journal, which covers a period of fifty-four years, is one of the most informative and accurate accounts of life on the Comstock.

On November 18, 1866, Doten wrote in his journal:

Some fellows took No. 1's engine about 4 o'clock this morning and washed out old Cad Thompson's whore house—gave her hell—created quite a consternation among the law and order portion of the community— —not the end of it yet— We shall have to see who rules the city now the rough or the decent men.

December 31, 1866, Doten notes that Thompson's place was known as "The Brick." which at this time was located on North D Street. The property on North D Street, known as 56 N. D Street [1878-79 City Directory] was sold by Thompson May 27, 1892 to Jacob Tucker for $20. The lot is listed as lot 5 of block 66. This was right across from the V and T freight depot. The lot is empty today, but nearby a large cottonwood grows.

July 4, 1867, Doten writes that John Dolton resisted arrest in Cad Thompson's and was shot and killed by Hawkins, a policeman. Only hours earlier, Zink Barnes was accidentally shot by Hugh Kerrin, fire Chief, at the same place.

Throughout the 1870's, Cad Thompson appears in the lists of uncalled for letters and on the arrival and departure lists from Virginia City. Now and then she was arrested for drunk and disorderly conduct.

The February 17, 1875 issue of the *Territorial Enterprise*, reveals Thompson's real name was Sarah Hagan. Andrew Allison took Hagan to court to repossess his house in the red light district. What the circumstances were are not clear. Hagan fought Allison bitterly for a month, but lost the case.

Thompson died in Virginia City, March 23, 1897. That day the Virginia City *Evening Chronicle* wrote this of Thompson:

Mrs. Caroline Thompson, commonly known as "Cad" Thompson, an historic Comstock "character", died this morning at her home on the corner of D street and Sutton Avenue...

The deceased settled on the Comstock in the early sixties, and during thirty odd years that followed, her name became well known all over the Coast through the events connected with her life and establishment. Her career was long and eventful, if notorious as well. She was born in Ireland, and according to her story, while still a girl, took 50 pounds belonging to an uncle and ran away to New York, where she had relatives.

From New York she went to California in the early fifties, where she met and took up with Thompson, who was a stock broker. Thompson held her out as his wife, though it is claimed they were never mar-

ried, and they lived together for several years, a son and a daughter being born to them. Eventually separating from Thompson, she came here.

She placed her children in Santa Clara college, and there they were educated, coming here during their vacations to visit her. After settling here she became the keeper of a fast house, and continued in this nefarious business till her death. Thompson [Cad's husband]...returned to New York after the separation, entered the banking business and married another woman.

Some twenty years ago, when her children were verging upon manhood and womanhood, the deceased went to New York to see Thompson. Then, as the tale goes...she demanded settlement of $20,000 for her children, threatening Thompson with prosecution for bigamy.

...Thompson refused point blank to meet the demand; whereupon...she drew a pistol, leveled at his head and threatened to kill him, and he changed his mind.

Not withstanding that "Cad" Thompson led a life of immorality and conducted a notorious establishment, she had some sterling qualities.. She was absolutely honest, and she was genuinely charitable. The business men of the Comstock say that her word in business matters was as good as gold, and her credit was of a character that enabled her to raise large sums of money whenever she wished.

During the twenty or thirty years which she lived on the lower street, she performed innumerable acts of real charity. There never was a case of sickness or destitution on the street that she did not provide for if it was brought to her notice...

The deceased owned the house where she lived but it was mortgaged for about $4000. She is said to have left about $2000 worth of diamonds and a thousand shares of stock, also. The diamonds, it is stated, were bequeathed to friends in a will that she left.

She said she was born under a respectable roof, and that she wished to die in the open air rather than in her house, but her wish was not carried out for some reason or other. She was between 65 and 70 years old, and leaves no known relatives. Her remains will be buried here, and be removed later to San Francisco possibly.

Thompson's adult daughter had died years ago. Eight or nine years earlier Thompson's son overdosed on morphine after several suicide attempts.

Rosa May about 1879. She was twenty-four and working brothels in Carson City and Virginia City, Nevada. Photo copyrighted Michael J. Williams.

122

Laura Davenport, fellow prostitute and friend of Rosa May's.
Photo copyrighted Michael J. Williams.

Virginia City, Nevada in the late 1870's. Photo is shot from the north. Arrow points to area on North D Street where Cad Thompson's "Brick house" brothel was located.

Top, rare photo of Cad Thompson's three story "Brick house" brothel on the left. Bottom, Virginia City cribs on D Street. Photo taken in the 1940's. Only one crib survives today. Photos copyright Michael J. Williams. All rights reserved.

First page of a letter to Rosa May from notorious brohtel madam, Cad Thompson, who was then in San Francisco. Rosa May was sometimes put in charge of Thompson's three story parlour house on D Street. Copyright Michael J. Williams.

Carson City about 1880 on a dark winter day. Photo was taken at the state capitol from the southeast. The two story bulding is the Ormsby House hotel at Carson and Second Streets. Arrow points to Ormsby Street and Carson red light district. Photo copyright Michael J. Williams.

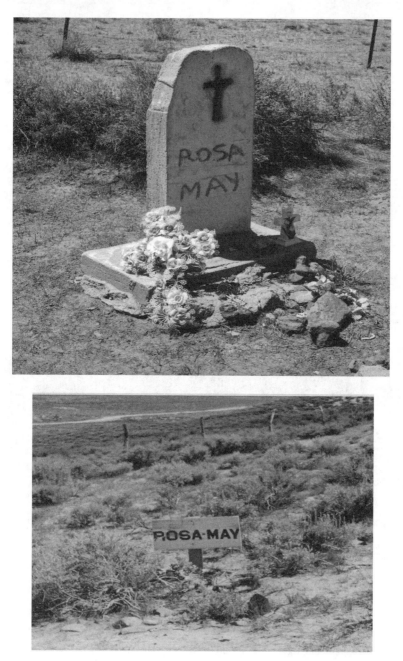

Top, Louis Serventi's gravestone made around 1965. Photo copyright Michael J. Williams. All rights reserved. Bottom, the sign that marked Rosa May's alleged grave about 1961. Photo courtesy Will P. Ralph.

Burton Frasher's 1927 photo of the Bodie cemetery showing Rosa May's picket fenced grave in the outcast cemetery .Courtesy Burton Frasher Jr..

Close-up photo of Rosa May's original grave site and fence. Courtesy Burton Frasher Jr..

Bodie about 1900. Arrow points to Rosa May's house in the redlight district. A.A. Forbes photo copyright Michael J. Williams.

Bodie about 1900. Arrow points to Rosa May's house. Men shown hauling equipment for cyanide milling of ore. Photo courtesy of Anthony Knapp.

Top, a rare photo of Rosa May's house, third on the right. Below, today the empty field in north Bodie where Rosa May's house once stood amongst other houses of prostitution. Arrow points to house site..

Bodie about 1927. Arrow points to Ernest Marks's saloon on the west side of Main Street. Courtesy Burton Frasher Jr..

Rosa May's handwritten letter that helped unlock the story of her life. Photo by Ron Brewer, copyrighted Michael J. Williams. All rights reserved.

A portion of a page from the 1910 U.S. census showing Rosa May was still alive in Bodie in 1910. The census agent listed Rosa May's age as "46,"--she was 55, that she was single, born in Pennsylvania and had lived at the address 8 years. Courtesy Linda Glick

A pencil written letter to Rosa May from "Emma" a fellow prostitute.

This could have been the dark and brooding winter scene as Rosa May's friends hauled her body on a sled to Bodie's outcast cemetery for burial. Photo copyrighted Michael J. Williams. All rights reserved.

Top, author George Willaims III replaces a version of Rosa May's original grave site fence. Bottom, an envelope mailed to Rosa May, then living in Carson City, courtesy Helen Evans. Photos copyrighted Michael J. Williams.All rights reserved.

Hugh McCaghren

To   Deed

Rosa May

This Indenture made the 14th day of June
in the year of our Lord one thousand nine hundred and two
Between Hugh McCaghren of the City and County of San
Francisco State of California the party of the first part and
Rosa May of Bodie Mono County State of California the
party of the second part. Witnesseth. That the said party
of the first part for and in consideration of the sum of One
hundred and seventy five $175.00 Dollars lawful money of the
United States of America to him in hand paid by the said
party of the second part the receipt whereof is hereby acknowledged
does by these presents remise release and forever Quitclaim unto
the said party of the second part and to her heirs and assigns
all that certain lot piece or parcel of land situate in the
town of Bodie County of Mono State of California and bounded
and particularly described as follows to wit. That certain
lot No 42 in Block No 26 . west side of Bonanza Street
as the same appears on the official map of the town of Bodie
Cal made by Leo A Scowden in 1880. Together with the
dwelling house and all improvements situate and erected on
said Lot No 42 Block No 26 aforesaid and whatever furniture
and fixtures belonging to and contained therein which said
dwelling house & improvements have been occupied by the
party of the second part upwards of 10 years as a residence
in said Bodie Cal.

Together with all and singular the tenements hereditaments
and appurtenances thereunto belonging or in any wise appertaining
and the reversion and reversions remainder and remainders rents

The grant deed to Rosa May's house in the Bodie red light district.
Photo copyrighted Michael J. Williams.All rights reserved.

140

Rosa May's redlight at the Bodie Museum. Photograph by Rick Lancaster courtesy of Gary Howard.

Chapter 10

As I sat in Helen Evans' living room, reading Rosa May's letters for the first time, I knew little of what I've shared. The letters were a window into a few years of Rosa's life. But for the time being, that window was fogged by the ornate Victorian script which made reading the letters difficult; it was fogged by unfamiliar expressions, unknown identities and strange subtleties.

Five months of research had quickly passed. What had at first seemed an easy task had become a mountain. And the work was only beginning. Hundreds of research hours would be required to decipher the letters. I would have to identify people mentioned in the letters; I had to learn what unfamiliar expressions meant. I would have to study the histories of Virginia City, Carson City and the entire Comstock Lode. I would need to understand the era to better understand the letters. A thorough knowledge of early California and Nevada history was imperative.

The letters were a key to Rosa's life. But only diligent research could provide the missing information I needed to establish an accurate portrait of Rosa's life.

Feeling somewhat overwhelmed by the work that lay ahead, I borrowed money, gathered my camping gear and headed back to Bodie. There, I hoped to get re-energized.

As I sped down from Dead Man's Summit on U.S. 395, Mono Lake stretched wide and blue. Beyond were the Bodie Hills. Dotted with pinon pines and sagebrush, the Hills lay green against the cold, autumn sky. Now the sun did not shine as brightly as it had in the summer. A fierce wind down from the Sierra buffeted my VW.

As I again crept over Cottonwood Canyon road up the Bodie Hills to the ghost town, the wild, pungent smell of sagebrush penetrated the car. I had missed the fragrance. It was the smell of the Wild West.

Bodie lay a silent ruin in the narrow, green valley. The

142

autumn cold had driven everyone but the park rangers away. Hands in my pockets, jacket snug around my neck, head down, I walked Bodie's deserted streets alone. I crept around the brown weathered buildings, again walked the back lots of trash and deserted wagons, climbed the hill to Rosa May's grave. There, as usual, I paused, hoping for an inspired revelation. None came.

I walked down the hill from the cemetery, across town and past the silent Standard Mill, down to Chinatown where Rosa had lived and died. The field was empty of summer tourists. Even the cattle were gone, taken from the high country at summer's end. At one end of the field, the jail sat quietly missing its once rowdy prisoners. A brick building lay crumpled in the middle of the field. A square outline of stones that once supported Rosa May's house—the Palace it was known as during boom years—lay like white, ancient bones. An icy wind came hard against my face. I walked back to my car through the wind. I was distressed. Bodie, the ghost town, with its eerie silence, could not give me the answers I sought. I was resigned. If Rosa's story could ever be found, it would be found in courthouse files and faded early newspapers; in ancient letters and memories of old timers.

Helen Evans had allowed me to reproduce Rosa May's photograph. The 8 x 10 black and white photo stood in its frame on my writing desk. Rosa's sensitive eyes stared back at me twenty-four hours a day. Sometimes I stared back. I had a feeling there was a more meaningful story somewhere in Rosa May's legend. At times I felt a presence of something or somebody trying to urge me forward.

I spent my days writing old-timers who had lived in Bodie. I re-read Rosa's letters countless times and made notes. There were books to read, articles to check. Slowly, little by little, fact by fact, Rosa May's story was coming together.

Over the next two and a half years my enthusiasm held up. I uncovered information in seven major ways:

1. Newspapers of the era brought Rosa's time to life. These newspapers included the Virginia City, *Territorial Enterprise*, the *Gold Hill News*, Carson *Morning Appeal*, *Bridgeport Chronicle-Union* and the *Bodie Miner*. Fortunately, some of these

newspapers had been preserved and were now on micro-film at the Nevada State Library in Carson City. I accessed them through inter-library loans.

It was thrilling to find Rosa's name on the railroad arrival/departure lists in Virginia City. Persons mentioned in the letters also turned up. With each newspaper, Rosa's time, her people and her town became more real. I came to know the merchants who sold to her, the policemen she avoided, the miners, pimps, whores and madams she had brushed arms with long ago.

2. Pacific Coast Directories and city directories helped to identify those mentioned in the letters.

3. Courthouse records in Bridgeport, Carson and Virginia City continued providing information.

4. State and Federal records, such as the 1875 Nevada Census and the 1870, 1880 and 1900 Federal Census helped to identify many. Passport records in Washington were also searched.

5. I managed to find more old-timers who had lived in Bodie while Rosa was alive. I drove to their cities and interviewed them. Each offered valuable bits of information.

6. Research reading covered California and Nevada history, with special attention given to Bodie, Carson and Virginia City.

7. Research of the history and causes of prostitution continued. Reading included books and articles by psychologists, sociologists, historians, prostitutes, pimps and madams.

I found several books which illuminated the prostitute's life and problems. In the following pages, Nell Kimball, a 19th century New Orleans madam, reveals her life as a parlor house prostitute and madam. Polly Adler, New York City madam of the 1920's, 30's, and 40's, discusses the girls who worked for her. And Harold Greenwald, psychoanalyst, summarizes his findings from interviews with twenty call girls. This information helps us to understand Rosa's May's life.

Chapter 11

The New Orleans madam Nell Kimball was born on a Missouri farm in 1854. (Rosa May was born in 1855.) Her large family was poor and her religious father was unsympathetic and hard. At fifteen Kimball ran away to St. Louis with a Civil War veteran to escape the hopelessness of her home life. Her boyfriend soon deserted her. With no money and no job, Kimball lived on the streets. She was determined not to go home.

She found work at Zig's, a high class parlor house. For the next ten years Kimball worked as a parlor house prostitute. Kimball confesses she was a confused young whore who didn't trust anyone and wanted nothing to do with love. In later years she realized she had wasted her youth.

At twenty-five she left Zig's when she married a bank robber. Her husband was killed two years later while committing a robbery. Kimball found herself a young widow with a child, and no means of living. She did not want to go back to prostitution and worked at carnival booths and factories for terribly low wages. She explains that working women were not respected during this period.

All alone working at low paying jobs, she struggled to make ends meet, and stay straight. Kimball neared emotional exhaustion. Then tragedy: her son died.

Embittered by the deaths of her husband and child, Kimball contemplated suicide, but decided to live. She returned to Zig's parlor house where she met a wealthy tobacco capitalist who kept her for several years until the wife discovered the relationship. Kimball left St. Louis with enough money to open her own house.

She settled in New Orleans and searched Storyville, the red light district, for a suitable house. In the 1890's the city had declared Storyville the official red light district and confined prostitution to that area.

Kimball found a two story house, filled it with fine furniture, beds and linen, hired a maid, bouncer, and five or six beauties. She paid off the local officials, and opened a high class parlor house that catered to successful professional men. She was a madam for nearly forty years until November 17,1917, when Storyville was officially closed by the Federal Government during World War I.

As Kimball tells it, there was never a shortage of willing girls who wanted to be prostitutes. Most had landed in the city as she had, with no money, no job, and no place to stay. It wasn't difficult convincing these girls of the advantage of a square meal and a place to sleep.

Kimball believed the unavailability of jobs for single and widowed women, and the low pay at sweat shops as the main reasons young women became prostitutes. Masters and Benjamin, authors of *Prostitution and Morality*, elaborate the poor girl's predicament in the late 19th century:

....it was well established that a large proportion of all prostitutes then came from the ranks of the domestic servants—in England and on the Continent, as well as in the United States. Prostitution and the domestic service (along, sometimes, with sweat-shop labor) were almost the only careers open to an unmarried girl of the lower classes, and the near starvation wages paid to servants, in combination with long working hours, grueling toil, and frequently, cruel treatment, would have made prostitution the obvious career choice for most of such women had prostitution been less harshly condemned by the society. As it was, many women preferred censure to a thankless and ill-paid servitude.

By mid 19th century men and women were leaving the farms and rural life for the city and factory work. They believed city life and factory work would free them from the drudgery of agricultural work. But without labor unions and organization, the city's newcomers lacked the clout to compel companies to pay higher wages. They found themselves at the mercy of powerful companies. Women earned far less than men for doing the same job for the same hours. There was a reason.

In the 19th century in Great Britain and America, the

man's role was family provider. It was offensive for a wife to work outside the home to help pay the bills. It was a woman's duty to bear and care for children and handle domestic chores. It was man's sole duty to provide. It was a man's world; working women were a threat to man's position. It followed, that a man's labors were worth more and he was paid better than women for the same job.

The unmarried woman and widow found themselves in a precarious plight. Without a man to provide support, a woman was dependent on low paying domestic or sweat shop labor. An unmarried woman was adrift and vulnerable. This made the easy wages of prostitution attractive.

In addition to the economic pressures, there were moral restraints which increased the need for prostitutes.

Queen Victoria and Prince Albert had a profound influence on the thinking of men and women in England, Europe and the United States. Queen Victoria has often been blamed for the austere morality of her reign. But it was her husband, Prince Albert, who actually advocated the idealistic and stern morality which became synonymous with the Victorian Era.

Victoria and Albert encouraged all men and women to live good wholesome lives, to strive for perfection, to try always to fulfill the Golden Rule. This led to the creation of a number of worthy social causes: orphanages, hospitals, and labor unions which helped increase wages.

But the austere morality had a very negative effect on sexual attitudes. Sex was regarded as a necessary physical act whose sole purpose was procreation. Sexual drives and feelings were considered the lust of the flesh and were to be repressed—even in marriage. Few married men saw their wives entirely naked.

Because of the sexual repression, men, having more freedom in society, began seeking out women with whom they could release their pent up sexual frustration. Since sexual passions were considered base and sinful, and not to be consummated with a "Good" woman—the future wife and mother—this led to a demand for a lower type of woman, the prostitute.

Prostitution fulfilled needs for both Victorian men and

women. For the Victorian male, it offered relief from sexual tensions. For thousands of poor women, it was a means to earn a living and achieve the material and creature comforts they otherwise would have been denied.

But prostitution was an awful blemish in the highly moral Victorian society. Its presence could not be ignored by decent men and women, especially when girls as young as ten or eleven were involved.

With the increase in prostitution, numbers of social reformers arose who tried to solve the problem. Some were religious people outraged by the increase in prostitution. Others were deeply troubled by the way poor women were forced to earn a living, destroying their bodies and spirits in the process.

Reformers tended to fall into two factions: 1) the Abolitionist, who sought to completely abolish prostitution and 2) the Regulationist, who believed prostitution was inevitable, the best course being its lawful regulation to check disease, and thereby protect innocent women and children.

Regulationists favored licensing prostitutes and establishing health clinics where prostitutes could be examined and treated for disease.

Abolitionists were appalled by this, for they believed the regulation of prostitution meant the acceptance of the social evil.

Regulationists and Abolitionists were unable to reconcile their differences and fought bitterly from 1860 until 1917, when wide open prostitution was outlawed in many cities. As a consequence, prostitution continued unregulated, causing widespread disease and the physical, emotional and spiritual destruction of thousands of women.

Ironically, the bantering among reformers and resulting newspaper publicity, brought prostitution ever more into the limelight, causing terrific stimulation for the skin trade.

The boom in prostitution brought more adamant pleas from the clergy and reformers for the reformation of man's "wicked ways." This led to the formation of the Purity Movement, 1885-1900, bent on the moral betterment of man, to be achieved by the internalizing and discipline to certain prescribed moral values. The Purity Movement, merely urged stricter self-control of sexual passions. It further increased sexual guilt and drove men to prostitutes in their attempts to rid themselves of guilt and sexual frustration. It appears that these reformers could not grasp the idea that God may have created sexual desires to insure the propagation of the human race.

All this had a profound influence on Nell Kimball's thinking as a 19th century woman, prostitute and madam. Her animosity and distrust of society were feelings developed over time by experience.

It began with her father, who preached love and mercy but was without feeling for his wife and children. Kimball learned to distrust religion and the social values religion advocates. Her father's hardness of heart left Kimball with emotional wounds that never healed.

Her budding bitterness was reinforced as a fifteen year old prostitute servicing the sexual needs of successful professional men with wives and children at home. Seeing society's best at their worst, made Kimball aware of society's hypocrisy.

Her bitterness grew as a young widow, as she struggled to go straight, while working for pauper's wages, barely able to support herself and her child.

Finally, as a madam for many years, forced to pay off bureaucrats, police and wealthy landlords, Kimball was convinced of society's hypocrisy and greed.

There was, therefore, a great bond among fellow prostitutes and madams. They saw themselves as women who were used sexually and profited from economically, upon whom were thrust society's lonely and unloved, violent and frustrated, women adored in the bedroom and mocked in the streets.

Though poor wages made prostitution attractive, Kimball admits there were other reasons girls became prostitutes. Some girls were fools who had no idea of what they were getting themselves into. Many were once singers, dancers and entertainers who really didn't have much talent. These fooled themselves. As soon as they made enough to buy new music or costumes, they'd get out of the racket. Most could never admit they were full time whores.

There were smart girls who liked the isolation and protection as a parlor house prostitute. Kimball explains, that such women were generally unhappy and afraid of the outside world. They tended to drink more than other whores.

Others girls liked the rebellious life style, easy money, fancy clothes, fine food and liquor. But for most, prostitution was just another way of making a living, earning enough for food and clothing and a bit of luxury. Most were ordinary people doing a job society would not admit there was a need. The only criterion for a good whore was a genuine desire to be one; a girl had to take pride in what she could offer a man.

Kimball ran a $20 house, $10 during depressions. Most houses usually opened at noon and closed in the early morning.

A girl could make between $50 and $200 a week. But most girls were always broke. (A common laborer at top pay, would have had to work ten weeks to make $200.) The girls spent their money on dressmakers, stockings, hats, perfume, ivory comb sets, jewels, things that weren't worth much when a girl had to pawn them.

Girls gave their money to their pimps who often got them hooked on drugs, mostly opium, using addiction as a means to control the girls.

The men these girls loved were the real trouble in their lives. The girls were often overly sentimental and easy to manipulate. They were depressed if they didn't have a steady man. Most had lost any sexual feeling except for their pimp. Yet even on this debased level, women needed love and this need kept them human. They often felt disgraced and looked down upon by their customers. There was a genuine desire to be respected as a human being. They turned to pimps for token love and occasional affection.

The occupational hazards and torment of the prostitute's life were insufferable. Consider one of her days:

She wakes in the early afternoon and comes downstairs for coffee. She never feels like eating much and the madam must force her to eat breakfast.

She sits or lies about during the afternoon, plays cards, gossips with the other girls. Usually she has no interests and may begin to drink. Sometimes she goes shopping, buys a new dress, hat, jewelry or perfume.

In the early evening, she dresses in a fine gown, but nothing too fancy. When the Johns arrive, the madam calls her and five or six other girls downstairs. The Johns may be repeat customers or strangers.

The girl goes into her act: she is sweet, she is pretty, she is dumb, she is willing, she has no needs, she is a servant, she'll do whatever any man wants.

She sits with the other girls beside their customers at the long mahogany dining table. The talk is gay; the other girls giggle, she giggles too. The men are buying and pouring champagne, $20 a bottle. The madam is charming, witty, strong, in control.

Dinner finished, the girls and Johns move into the parlor. There is a bar where a brawny bouncer serves as bartender. The girls and Johns sip drinks. She is gay and cool as she makes her hustle. Finally, one of the men chooses her.

She leads him up the stairs by the hand, one hand on the banister, to her room and the big bed. She does anything he wants, and says anything he wants her to say. If the John is a repeat customer, she knows his needs and goes about her business self-assured. This is one thing in life she does well. She moans, but she is not aroused. It is all an act, but it is thoroughly convincing. As she goes through the motions, she hopes he will climax soon so she can get on to the next customer. But she does not rush him, bad business; it would hurt his feelings and ruin his tip.

It's over. She washes the John down with hot water and soap. If he picks up anything, he'll know he didn't get it from her. She smiles and jokes as she washes. The John is drunk and feels relieved after the workout. She helps him dress. As he leaves he palms a gold coin on her dresser. She smiles and thanks him.

Immediately she begins to douche. There are several to choose from: lysol, bichloride of mercury, mercuric cyanide, carbolic acid and potassium permanganate. Afterwards, she dresses and combs her hair. The maid rushes in to change the sheets and makes the bed for the next John.

Meanwhile, the John has gone downstairs and the madam has graciously collected the $20, part of which belongs to the girl. The madam asks if he is pleased. He is. The John may leave but more often stays to visit with other Johns, many of whom he knows or does business with.

The parlor house is sort of a social club; the men meet often, sometimes just to visit the girls and other men. Sometimes the men play poker, but the girls try to steer them away from gambling. They know men prefer gambling to sex.

The girl comes downstairs and hustles another customer. She may hustle as many as twenty or thirty a night and rarely will one arouse her. She may work as late as five or six in the morning. Sometimes a John will stay the night. If none stay and work is done, she goes out with her pimp or with other girls to a restaurant. Over food and drinks, the girls talk about their various customers, especially the strange ones.

If the girl has a pimp, she'll hand over most of her night's earnings. If she has done well, the pimp is pleased and treats her kindly. If she hasn't done well, he may beat, scold, or deny her affection. She tries to do well so her pimp will be pleased and be nice to her. Her pimp is everything to her, her God, her master, her lover. As strange as it seems, her relationship with him is the most important human contact she has.

If the girl does not have a pimp, she's probably blue. All night, men have pawed and used her and not one has given a damn about her. She may start to drink hard, snuff "snow" (cocaine) or take laudanum, a liquid preparation of opium, to comfort her loneliness. If she goes low enough, she may kill herself, which is not uncommon. If not, she returns to the house, sleeps until the next afternoon, waking to repeat the same routine that hardly ever changes. She is off one day a week to spend with her pimp or go where she likes. She is like a little girl living at home under strict rules. Responsibility for her life is put in someone else's hands, at least temporarily.

Such was the parlor whore's routine, years without thought, planning or meaning. It was a rare girl, who, after some years in the trade, lived a normal, happy life. Many were constantly depressed, eventually cracked up or killed themselves. Suicide was a haunting demon in every whorehouse.

The loneliness of a prostitute's life, even the high class

parlor house girl, was immense. Cut off from her family by disgrace, the resulting shame and loneliness was awesome. She had put herself in a world where she was used by everyone: customers, madams, pimps, and often lesbian lovers.

To add to her troubles, there was the constant threat of pregnancy or disease, Little Casino (gonorrhea) or Big Casino (syphilis.) And there were always the crazies: overly polite men who cracked their knuckles and beat or killed prostitutes when they had the chance.

The life was hard on a girl and wore her down physically, emotionally, mentally and spiritually. Unlike other professions, a prostitute's money making years were few. She started at top pay and earnings decreased as her youth and beauty faded. At best, a girl lasted a half dozen years in a quality parlor house. After that, she usually became a street hooker, whispering arousing offers to passersby, exposing herself on street corners.

The parlor house girl, who had been protected by the madam, was well fed and clothed, and known the best customers, found street hustling extraordinarily humiliating. As Dolly Fine, another madam, once said, "There is nothing more pitiful in life than a prostitute who has risen from the streets, tasted luxuries and liked them, and then finds herself once again in the gutter." Rather than live with the fall, many fading prostitutes killed themselves.

Polly Adler's autobiography, *A House Is Not A Home*, a best seller, provides more insight into the lives of prostitutes through the eyes of an intelligent, observant woman. Adler was a New York City madam in the 1920's, 30's and 40's. Though a madam of more recent years, Adler's observations often parallel Kimball's.

Like Kimball, Adler had no trouble procuring girls. Quite the opposite, "...far from having to lure girls there, I was forced to turn away 30 or 40 for every one I was able to accommodate."

Many who knocked on her door were not cut out for the hard life of prostitution. Adler persuaded them to go home. The girls she hired were experienced, willing and eager. She did not hire novices. All her girls were pretty, had good health and were clean.

Most prostituted themselves for money. There were a few who did it for kicks; there were always a few extremists who loved whoring. At the other extreme were girls who detested the life, girls who gave customers smiles while hating them.

Adler admits, "For 99 out of 100 girls, going to bed with a customer was a joyless, even distasteful experience."

Most of the girls were of average intelligence. None had any intention of staying in the business. Most were aware a career in prostitution was short lived and reserved for the young. The smart ones saved for retirement. Most did not. They squandered their money and used this as an excuse to stay in the life. Most made no preparation for the future. Some didn't know when to quit; others wouldn't try anything else.

Some were talented—actresses, dancers, singers. They spent their days working at their craft. The majority, however, spent their time at the beauty parlor, at the movies or played cards, hearts their favorite. The reason they didn't do much in their off hours, Adler explains, was because of their strenuous work. After eight or ten hours of mental and physical exercise, they had no desire to exert themselves.

"Inevitably I had a few lesbians, some of them troublemakers, some very peaceful souls. It's often been said that a prostitute becomes so tired of being mauled by men that she turns to a woman for tenderness. Maybe so. I have no figures on the incidence, but it's my observation that it occurs in every walk of life."

"I have said my girls were go-getters, but it wasn't only because of the money that they liked to keep busy. It was also an escape from thinking. Even the least introspective could not always avoid recognizing the precariousness of her position and the loneliness of it. By becoming a prostitute, a girl cuts herself off not merely from her family, but from such a great part of life. She is isolated not just by social custom but by working conditions, and she has to some extent deprived herself of her rights as a citizen for which she has forfeited the protection of the law. It is not syphilis which is the occupational disease of the prostitute but loneliness."

Loneliness was worst on holidays, especially Christmas

and New Years. Many of the girls had sent family gifts. By New Year's they were down in the dumps. They hadn't received so much as a thank you note.

New Year's was the worst holiday because it was a time for planning for the future. "Most prostitutes," Adler explains, "try to avoid thinking of the future and the passing time...Youth is their capital. For a whore, New Years is a season of regret for the past rather than one of hope for the future."

Adler believed a prostitute could count on no more than ten money making years. "Then she is through—if not dead or diseased, so broken by drugs, alcohol and the steady abuse of her body that no one will hire her again."

All her girls were sentimental, and to escape their loneliness, went to clubs to hear crooners sing sad songs. Many hid tears as the singers sang torch songs, for their love lives were often unhappy. Many had pimps who mistreated them.

Adler, like Kimball, had no great love for pimps: "I cannot deny that I mortally hate pimps. Still, in the long run, they are also victims—though not so obviously or so pitifully—along with the girls they exploit. Most of them come from poverty-stricken homes, and they acquire their education in the streets and in the pool halls, first out front, then in the back room. Their only talent seems to be that they have a way with women, and they find this out hanging around the dance hall chippies, the drugstore waitress and the high school sweater girls who flaunt their sex and ask for attention."

"The pimp doesn't feel that he's doing wrong in putting his girls to work. He and the girls are in it together to trim the suckers. He thinks of himself as a smart operator, and sees nothing shameful in exploiting women and living on their earnings. (To his mind, all men exploit women to some degree.) He regards himself as an employer or a property owner, not as a criminal or a parasite. He considers that in taking over certain responsibilities for his girls, managing them, booking them into houses, getting them out of jail, and teaching them the ropes, he earns the money the girls give him. He dins it into each gin that if she wants to survive she must give him unquestioning obedience. In return for the money she makes (which he teaches her she could not earn without him) he listens to her complaints and is kind to her, when he has the patience and when she has earned enough to satisfy him. Since these girls almost never find men who care for them—what man wants to love a prostitute?— their relationship with the pimp constitutes the only important human tie they have. Just as the prostitute never, until the very end, is able to perceive that she is the victim, so the pimp never regards himself as exploited. He would be thunderstruck if it were pointed out to him that he has a miserable life, despised by other men, by madams he meets and deals with, by the under- world and by society. He thinks he is a very clever character, a sharp guy, able to make a buck and put up a front...the average pimp becomes an alcoholic and/or a drug addict, and in his last days a panhandler."

If prostitution was such an awful life, what drove girls into it in the first place?

Adler: "In my opinion the single factor—and the com- mon denominator in an overwhelming majority of cases—is poverty. It is true that, though many girls are poor, only a small percentage of them take to hustling. But there is more than one kind of poverty— there is emotional poverty and intellectual poverty and poverty of the spirit. As well as material lacks, there can be a lack of love, a lack of education, a lack of hope. And out of such impoverishment the prostitute is bred."

In an effort to discover the causes of prostitution, Harold Greenwald, a psychoanalyst, conducted intensive interviews with twenty call girls. His findings differed only slightly from Polly Adler's. Emotional impoverishment seemed to be the great- est cause of prostitution.

Of the twenty prostitutes Greenwald interviewed, not one came from a home where there a was a permanent, well adjusted marriage. Not one admitted growing up in a happy home where parents got along. In seventy-five percent of the cases, homes were broken up by adolescence. In the remaining cases, the girls never saw sympathy or affection between parents.

Two girls had parents that went through three divorces; three girls came from families where there were six divorces; six girls saw their mothers living with men to whom they were not married. Because of the absence of warmth and permanence in their families, these girls were unable to form an attachment to either parent, and hence, were unable to absorb society's values which we most often acquire from parents to whom we feel close.

The general attitude of these parents toward their children seemed to be one of complete rejection. The girls were rejected by fathers who didn't care about them, left home or died, or by mothers who never let them forget how much they had sacrificed for them. Nineteen of the twenty girls admitted feeling rejected by both parents.

Additionally, many were thrown from one home to the next. Three girls were passed from family to family; three from one foster home to another; four lived in a succession of boarding schools.

From such a background of emotional neglect and rejection, half the girls had engaged in early sexual activity for which they were rewarded. They learned early they could barter sexual favors for affection and attention. By doing so, they temporarily overcame feelings of loneliness and unworthiness while at the same time expressing hostility toward parents for having neglected them.

Chapter 12

On the morning of June 1, 1900, Cecil Burkham, who ran Burkham's Dry Goods in Bodie and operated a stage between there and Hawthorne, Nevada, began walking each of Bodie's dirt streets, knocking on doors and asking questions. Burkham had been hired by the Federal Government to record the 1900 Federal Census of Bodie Township. It took Cecil Burkham sixteen days at fifty persons per day to record each of Bodie's eight hundred citizens.

On June 6, nearing the end of his rounds, he walked up King Street through Chinatown, went north at Bonanza Street, then down a slight incline. There were only three little white houses on Bonanza Street. He knocked on her door, feeling a bit embarrassed to be doing so in plain daylight. A stout, dark haired woman, unaccustomed to daytime visitors, opened the door. She was tired and answered Burkham's questions quietly.

Burkham carefully wrote down her answers near the bottom of his tally sheet. Name: Rosa May. Head of household. White female. Born January, 1855. Forty-five years old. Birthplace: Pennsylvania. Parents: Irish, born in Ireland. Embarrassed, Burkham listed her occupation as "seamstress," then a common misnomer for prostitute. She had been employed twelve months. She was able to read, write and speak English, and she rented her house.

Burkham asked if anyone lived with her. She lied. She said, no. Cecil Burkham thanked her and went to the two remaining houses on Bonanza Street. Chinamen lived in the two houses; Burkham wrote their answers down quickly. Finished with his quota, he shut the census docket and walked back to his store on Main Street for lunch.

On a blistering July day, nearly a year after I began my search, I drove to the National Archives and Service Center at Laguna Niguel, California. There I found Rosa May listed in the 1900 Federal Census of Mono County, California. The census provided the first recorded information regarding Rosa May and answered several important questions.

For one, the census proved that Rosa May was alive June 6, 1900. This contradicted Serventi's gravestone which stated Rosa May died in 1880. The fact that Rosa May had died after June 6, 1900, made it more likely that people who knew Rosa May might still be alive.

Second, the census information showed there were twenty fewer years in which records could have been destroyed, records located somewhere that might provide some insight into Rosa's life.

Third, the 1900 Census finally gave Rosa's obscure life a place and time of beginning: Pennsylvania, January, 1855. Unfortunately, the census did not specify the city or county of birth, information that would have helped. Knowing Rosa was born in 1855, I was able to determine that between 1876-80, when she lived in Carson and Virginia City, she was between twenty-one and twenty-five years of age.

In 1900, twenty years later, she was forty-five and still in prostitution.

Fourth, the census proved another part of Ella Cain's story was untrue. Rosa May was not French and she was not born in Paris. She was Irish, born of Irish immigrants somewhere in Pennsylvania.

Carefully studying the Bodie census, I discovered that on June 6, 1900, Rosa May was the only woman living in the Chinatown and red light district. Of the town's 800 men, women and children, there were 235 single men and but 50 single women including elderly widows. That meant five men for every single woman. Rosa May, perhaps the only prostitute in town at the time, certainly had a overwhelming business.

The 1900 census also corroborated information I had discovered earlier. Richie Conway remembered delivering milk to Rosa May in 1902. There was now proof that Rosa May was alive in 1900, making Richie's recollection accurate.

In addition, Sadie Cain, whom I had recently interviewed, said she saw Rosa May rocking on her porch around 1904-05.

And Anna McKenzie, whom I spoke of earlier, saw Rosa

May between 1908-10.

From this information, I now believed Rosa May could have lived as late as 1910, making her fifty-five at death.

Over the next several years, other facts would emerge. Early newspapers would help to identify the people and events of Rosa May's life. But the most important and revealing information would come from Rosa May herself. It happened like this:

Mary Ann Phillips ran a brothel on the southwest corner of 4th and Ormsby Streets in Carson City. She had bought the large two story place from Jennie Dupey for $3,350, December 5, 1874. That was quite a large sum at the time. A miner earning top pay would have to work five years, and saved all he earned to purchase the same house. Phillips, then fifty-three, a mother with a family, knew the house was a wise investment. The great silver bonanza had recently been discovered in Virginia City. A house in Carson City was ideal. Scores of men were employed at the Carson wood yards and silver mills. There was the State Legislature and the travelers who passed through Carson on their way to Virginia City.

About five o'clock in the afternoon of August 12, 1879, twenty-four year old Rosa May left Phillips' place with her beat-up leather bags in hand. Her trunk would be sent up later. Times were hard on the Carson girls now that Virginia City's mines were on the decline. More men were being laid off with each week. Rosa's stay at Mary Ann Phillips' house had not gone well. The girls had to walk the streets to drum up trade. Money was tight; times were not like they had been several years earlier when the men had jobs. Believing more money could be made in Virginia City, Rosa was now on her way back.

At five o'clock, the late afternoon sun still beat hard on Carson City. Rosa felt drops of perspiration trickle from her armpits and down her sides as she walked the ten blocks to the V and T depot at Carson and Washington streets. She dropped her bags every block or so to wipe the sweat from her forehead before the salty drops slid into her eyes.

At the V and T depot, she bought a ticket for two dollars and spent two hours on the train as it twisted back and forth up the mountain switch-backs to Virginia City. She smelled the burning pine wood through the train window all the way back to Virginia.

The train passed through Gold Hill, then over the Divide and into Virginia City. The depot was located at the corner of Union and D streets, in the middle of the red light district. Rosa May walked a block from the depot to Cad Thompson's brothel at 18 South D Street, on the west side of D between Union and Taylor, about the middle of the block. Thompson's place was a wooden two story building she rented though Thompson although owned the "Brick" at 56 North D Street

On the morning of August 18, 1879, Rosa May sat down at a desk at Cad Thompson's. She'd gotten up especially early to take care of some business before the other girls awoke and disturbed her. By mid-morning, Thompson's was already stifling hot. Rosa wiped sweat from her forehead and thought of the money.

Taking a sheet of baby-blue paper from the drawer, she dipped her quill into a small jar of dark blue ink. Rosa wrote a quick letter to Leo Miller, a jeweler and one of her best customers. She hoped Miller was still in town. She explained to him that she was back at Cad Thompson's and asked if he would visit her. She carefully addressed his letter and laid it beside the other letters she would mail to her best customers.

Finished with her writing, Rosa bundled the letters together and walked up D Street to Union, then up the hill to C Street and mailed them at the Post Office. She walked back down to Thompson's, smiling to herself, hoping her best customers would soon call.

Unfortunately, Leo Miller had left Virginia City. Several days later his letter was returned to Rosa, who, no doubt, was disappointed. But Rosa's disappointment would prove an invaluable asset in uncovering her story.

By an incredible stroke of fate, Leo Miller's letter was mistakenly kept by Rosa among her love letters for more than thirty years. If Rosa had destroyed Miller's letter on its return, or if she had discarded the letter in the intervening years, not a trace of her handwriting would have survived. Rosa's story would have remained a secret. For it was Rosa's May's handwriting that revealed Rosa May's character, that she was indeed the self-sacrificing woman legend claimed.

A friend who was interested in my search, made me aware of the importance of Rosa May's handwriting. She had studied graphoanalysis briefly and learned that handwriting analysis is able to reveal personality and motivations. She gave me several books on graphoanalysis which I read and studied for several months.

At first I was skeptical. But I was willing to give the science a chance for the sake of whatever information it might reveal about Rosa May.

After several months of study, I began to apply what I had learned by doing brief graphoanalyses on friends and strangers. Using the basics of graphoanalysis, I was surprised at how much I could learn about a person's character through their handwriting. This convinced me of the credibility of graphoanalysis. I then sought out professional graphoanalysts.

Photographs of Rosa's handwriting were examined by graphoanalysts Judy Craig, of Riverside, California, and Verna Lea Turner of Bakersfield, California. Both graphoanalysts agreed, that an absolutely thorough analysis of Rosa's personality was impossible based on the small amount of writing. In spite of this obstacle, both graphoanalysts— miles apart and without knowledge of the other— reached similar conclusions regarding Rosa's personality and life.

In addition, Judy Craig analyzed Ernest Marks's handwriting.

Rosa May was twenty-four when she wrote Leo Miller in Virginia City. She was a pretty, bright-eyed, petite young woman, with soft, curly brown hair and fair skin. She was a woman, graphoanalysts assured, who took particular interest in her appearance. She would have dressed neatly at all times, taking extra care with her hair, makeup, nails, etc. She was an attractive woman and would have drawn the attention of both men and women.

Rosa May had a likeable personality. She was a real

charmer, and used this talent to get what she wanted. She was very emotional and responded to people and situations immediately, without thought. She was quick to laugh at a joke and the first to shed tears when a sad story was told. She was irrepressible—very herself, most often friendly, talkative, with a wonderful sense of humor.

She was thoughtful, and took an interest in others. She was warm and good hearted. She would have never intentionally harmed anyone.

She was frank and would tell the truth as she saw it. She was loyal, both to people and ideas. She generally did not run from problems, but was flexible and would adjust—and in the end, stubbornly resist.

She carried herself with a certain stubborn pride and dignity. She might have been a whore, but people would respect her as a human being.

She was intelligent, logical, always making plans, but did not always rely on her good judgement. Her impulsiveness caused her to do or say things without thinking.

She had a number of negative personality traits that impeded her life, and very likely were reasons which led her into prostitution. These qualities are often found in the personalities and backgrounds of the compulsive-neurotic prostitute.

Though Rosa seemed happy and well adjusted to others, she was prone to great anxiety. Like many prostitutes, she had poor self-esteem. She felt poorly about herself. This led Judy Craig to conclude, that very likely Rosa had an unhappy childhood. There was evidence that Rosa had been made to feel poorly about herself very early in life. Also, it appeared she had grown up in an extremely strict home. Being an intelligent, free spirited woman, Rosa had resented the sternness and restrictions. She could think for herself and did not always agree with her parent's ideas. There was evidence that they had demanded that she accept their ways and she had resisted this. Rosa had deeply resented their control.

Ironically, as a prostitute, she had continued the pattern of being controlled by others. She was now controlled by pimps, madams, customer's needs and circumstances.

Rosa May's parents were Irish immigrants— likely farmers from southern Ireland. More than a million Irishmen fled Ireland during the potato famine 1845-50. Ninety percent of Ireland was Catholic. This may help to explain the overly-strict home in which Rosa grew up. For Irish Catholicism, had been negatively influenced by Jansenist priests. Jansenists advocated a fanatical suppression of sexual feelings. Women, for instance, were told to bathe clothed to avoid the "mortal sin" of seeing their naked bodies. Such ideas created tremendous guilt in regards to normal sexual feelings. Jansenism was a religious leftover from the Middle Ages.

From her handwriting, it seems that Rosa was not allowed to challenge the harsh beliefs her mother and father upheld. No doubt, this lack of freedom eventually led Rosa to leave home—and in later years, helped to cause tremendous confusion in regards to morality.

Rosa May's low self-esteem caused her to fear criticism. For instance, though she was quite intelligent, and capable of making her own decisions, she was indecisive, afraid to say "yes" or "no" and mean it. She lacked faith in herself and her abilities. Without faith in herself, she had little ambition. Circumstances or other people would control her.

Compounding this, was her confusion in regards to morality. Rosa May did not know right from wrong. There was little evidence in her handwriting that she had a moral code to guide her. I had felt this myself while reading Marks' letters.

Combined with her lack of morality, was a nature that was quite susceptible to temptations. She lacked self-control in some instances. Nor was she concerned about her reputation. Verna Lea Turner concluded—without my telling her so—that Rosa May was immoral and likely a prostitute.

Rosa, then, at twenty-four, was living in a strange half-world, without laws or direction. Yet, she was desperately seeking someone or something to guide her life. Lacking faith in herself, and a code of ethics to help her judge between right and wrong, Rosa could have easily been talked into conclusions by pressure or persuasion. Here was a confused young girl perfect prey for pimps and madams.

Judy Craig believed somewhere between Rosa's old life under her parents and her new life as a prostitute, something traumatic had happened. It may have been an unhappy home life that led to a bad marriage or bitter love affair. She may have been smooth talked into prostitution by a pimp or madam. Whatever, there was Craig believed a missing "link" between Rosa's former life and her present as a prostitute.

Rosa May had willingly placed herself in a hard world in which she could be exploited, beaten, robbed, murdered or generally abused. It was an extremely painful world in which no one could be trusted.

For Rosa, this world made perfect sense. Through her parents' lack of love she had learned that people betray. If one's parents couldn't be trusted, no one could. She had merely continued the pattern she had learned as a child. So she was an extremely cautious woman for all her outward charm. She was quite selective with whom she became close; there were perhaps one or two she may have somewhat trusted. And of these, she was terribly jealous of their time and affections. Marks's letters show this to be true.

In general, she was distrustful and feared rejection. She kept people at bay, and because of this, she was very lonely. The distance Rosa put between herself and others accounts for her living in Carson City much of the time, while Marks lived in Gold Hill, some twenty miles away.

Still, in her dealings with others, Rosa most often acted friendly, though she had a fault finding nature and allowed others to get on her nerves. At such times when she suspected imposition-and there were many-she would lose her temper and release a hoard of cutting barbs. But her anger would not last long and her fits of temper were curbed by her tact, diplomacy and sense of humor.

A loner by nature, she coveted her privacy. Suspicious and distrustful, she needed more space than most people. Since she was so outgoing, there would be times when she needed to be alone simply to recover from emotional outlay. During these times she felt emotionally exhausted, gloomy, disgusted, indifferent, even despairing. But she would recover once she had rested.

Though Rosa could have worked with others, she worked better alone or with a small group- such as the usual five or six girls in a brothel. Her fault finding, narrow-mindedness, and suspicious nature could at times make her difficult and troublesome. This likely got her fired by madams—or drove customers away.

All in all, she was a simple woman and did not want a great deal from life, a roof over her head, food, affection, enough money to meet immediate needs. Like most prostitutes, she lived for the moment. She was sensitive, earthy and appreciated the little things that make life meaningful.

Her interests tended toward good books, good music, the theater, art, music, etc. She was dexterous and had artistic talent. She may have drawn, painted, did needle work or played a musical instrument. It is interesting to note, that in the winter of 1877, an R. May was going door to door in Virginia City selling prints of the works of Antonio Conova, a 19th century sculptor.

Rosa was an independent woman and enjoyed traveling. Considering her emotional problems, her lack of motivation, her natural charm, for Rosa May prostitution was an ideal life.

One more thing: Rosa May was easily tempted to share and help others, even at a sacrifice to herself. She could very easily have been the good hearted prostitute who died trying to save stricken miners, as the Bodie legend claims.

In 1879, Ernest Marks was twenty-four, about 5'7," medium build, dark complected, dark eyes, dark hair. He was a German Jew and had immigrated to America with his family in 1866 when Marks was eleven. The family later settled in Gold Hill. He had at least one brother, Morris, and one sister. His father was an alcoholic

An analysis of his writing shows that Ernest Marks was a real hell raiser, a domineering man with a vicious temper, and quite capable of violence. He over-indulged himself in everything; he drank too much, had sex too much; ate too much. When Judy Craig asked me how old Marks was, she was stunned when

166

I told her, twenty-four. Here was a man, she said, whose health was that of a middle aged man who had spent his life abusing his body with too much drink and sex, whose nerves were totally shot. Decadent described his life style.

He was a tormented, storm of a man, moody, over-sensitive, unstable, terrified of criticism and rejection, and yet, exceedingly rebellious. He tried desperately to control his strong sexual and drinking appetites, but was terribly unhappy with himself for his inability to do so.

This guy couldn't be trusted; he was a con- artist, a user, whose friends were likely criminals. This man was out for himself and would do whatever he had to, to get what he wanted. This guy was dangerous.

Like Rosa May, Marks was confused. His confusion was caused in part by his involvement with many varied projects and activities. Though he started many projects, he was weak willed and couldn't finish them. He was a quitter. He would get what he wanted in life by manipulating and playing upon the weaknesses and vices of others.

When this guy didn't get his way, he would use diplomacy, try to smooth talk his way. When that didn't work, his temper would explode. There would be violence. This was a man a woman would be smart to fear. He could have physically abused Rosa.

Together, Marks and Rosa had an interesting relationship. Marks fulfilled the authoritarian figure Rosa needed. Marks was domineering and had no problem telling Rosa what to do, which satisfied her.

Yet ironically, Marks was far more unstable and unpredictable than Rosa, who was more even tempered. Marks was everything Rosa should have naturally wanted to avoid. She couldn't trust people and Marks was a man who couldn't be trusted. The fact that she chose to be with such a man, fit perfectly. A woman who has learned that all people betray, naturally chooses the most untrustworthy man to reinforce her misconception.

Marks and Rosa had several things in common. Both were strategists who would have stimulated themselves by trying to outwit each other. Both liked an argument and were good in arguments. Both were loners and coveted their privacy. Both were self-conscious and feared rejection; they shunned society, kept to themselves, and avoided responsibilities. Though they were intelligent and had enough talent to do something meaningful with their lives, they would have rather not tried, than try and fail.

Both had artistic talent. Marks had literary talent and Rosa could have drawn, acted or played a musical instrument. Both were interested in culture and would have enjoyed a good book, a play or music.

Unfortunately, both lacked direction, and a sense of purpose. For this reason they would exploit or depend upon others for whatever they wanted in life.

Chapter 13

I continued hustling my songs to Hollywood music publishers, making appointments and dragging my guitar into the high rises on Sunset Boulevard where I sang for the men with gold records in their eyes. My belief in my songs had grown in proportion to the work I had put into my songwriting. Now when I was turned down, I didn't walk away crushed. I believed in my songs and in my ability to write better songs with time and work.

My reputation as a strong songwriter had spread quickly among Hollywood publishers. This greased the rails and made it easier to make appointments.

I now focused on landing a staff songwriting deal. Some music publishers hire songwriters on staff. These publishers will pay a weekly wage to songwriters like a regular job. The wages are paid out against future royalties. When a songwriter's song begins making money, the publisher takes out of royalties the wages he has paid the songwriter. Being a staff songwriter helps the struggling songwriter pay rent and food.

I was finally offered a staff songwriting job by a well known publisher whose founders were very successful American songwriters. I would be paid $125 a week to write songs. Doesn't seem like much now, but this was when a dollar was worth something. The publisher and I shook hands to seal the deal. The publisher's lawyer would draw up the papers. The rep would call me on Monday.

I anxiously waited for his call on Monday. He didn't call. I waited Tuesday, Wednesday, then Thursday. Finally on Friday I called the publisher. Things had changed, he said. The deal had fallen through. "But we shook hands," I said. "Yeah, but things have changed," he said. "Well, they haven't changed with me," I said. "I was counting on this deal." There was no deal. He was sorry.

I had told friends and family that I'd been hired as a staff writer. Now I looked like a fool.

There were other disappointments but I will not bore you. I continued making appointments and driving into Hollywood and meeting with reps. Afterwards, emotionally drained, I drove back to Pasadena, often praying I would not run out of gas. I had spent my last dollar on a hamburger. Getting home, I checked the mail; a telephone bill and more returned tapes from publishers. Climbing the stairs, living on refried beans, corn tortillas and medium-hot salsa. How would I pay the phone bill, and now the rent was due. The night and the night worries. Did I really have talent as a songwriter, or was I fooling myself? Feeling uncertain, afraid, sometimes walking Colorado Boulevard for hours, that long street the Rose Parade meanders down each year across America's television sets. But there was no parade in the night. Just the city lights and other troubled men and women walking the night. I walked home, feeling uncertain, reaching for the phone in the early morning hours, calling a friend for reassurance, sometimes breaking down, my friend tried to reassure me.

I continued working at the pizza parlor serving beer and pouring root beers for high school girls with braces and two big, red pimples in the middle of their foreheads, and each girl with the eternal question: How much is a large root beer?—and the prices right in front of them.

I had had enough. I quit and began writing lead sheets for a major publisher when they had work. Suddenly, there was no more work and no more money and I was tired of being broke.

I moved back to Riverside and landed a five night a week gig. I had promised myself I would not work in bars to earn a living. Now there I was, and grateful to have the gig and a steady income.

Two weeks later a pretty, petite blonde came into the club where I was performing. Her name was Edie. She had an amazing resemblance to Rosa May. Four months later we were married. We bought a house and I was finally settled down.

My wife encouraged me to continue my Rosa May research, and began helping me. We spent part of our honeymoon in Bodie where I led Edie to Rosa May's outcast grave and showed her the open field where Rosa's house had stood. We pitched our tent in the campground just north of the field. The September nights high in the Bodie Hills were already freezing and we were cold in our sleeping bags in the night but my wife did not complain. We spent the remainder of our honeymoon doing research in Bridgeport, Carson City, Virginia City, Sacramento and San Francisco.

Over the next two years there were many research trips and my wife helped on all of them. We spent summer vacations in the Eastern Sierra and studied the history of the region, often camping in Bodie for several days at a time. The Bodie nights were always cold and we shivered in our sleeping bags, clinging to one another for warmth as the fresh mountain air came in through the tent window.

We grew to love the ghost town and the Bodie Hills. Standing on a mountain top, you could see for miles in every direction, the sky a smog-less royal blue. It was easy to understand why men and women came to this region and stayed. They must have loved the sweet smelling sagebrush as we did, especially after the summer storms when thunderheads came fast on the wind and the rain fell full and hard, and afterwards the air smelled of the damp sage and wet earth. We loved that as we had loved the mountain flowers and learning their names: the red Indian paintbrush, blue lupine, the fried-egg flowers, wild buckwheat, wild irises and the yellow blooming rabbit brush.

We spent many hours in the courthouses and museums of Bridgeport, Carson City and Virginia City, checking and re-checking land records, police records, court records, births and deaths, coroner inquests, city directories—all in hopes of finding more information about Rosa May. It was tedious work but it was satisfying work, and satisfying when we found what were looking for. We chased down every clue, hoping to find a fact in the end. Most of the chasing was fruitless, but there were those times when we gleaned a new fact and another piece of Rosa May's puzzle was set in place.

Carson City and Virginia City, were especially important to us, for these were where Rosa May had spent much time. When winter came, and we could not afford research trips, and I had to write down what we had learned in the summer, we treasured memories of time spent in Carson and Virginia City. We remembered walking down Carson' Ormsby Street and the huge cottonwoods that shaded us from the sun as we searched and found the houses where Rosa May had long ago lived and worked. We remembered how tired we became after hours in the Carson Courthouse, when we had to break, driving down to the Carson River, and the water that came as far as our knees, and Harvey, our Springer Spaniel, swimming in the river with three boys, playing with them though they were strangers, and afterwards the boys building a fire beside the river to warm themselves.

In Virginia City we remembered walking down the creaking boardwalks, visiting the old saloons, especially the Delta Saloon, where a century earlier, Ernest Marks, Rosa's young lover, had spent much time. Later, walking down D Street to the old red light district to the cottonwood tree across from the Virginia and Truckee freight depot, where Cad Thompson's "Brick house" brothel had stood. There was a full moon that night and the bright silver light lit up D Street and the backs of saloons where stairs led down to the red light. We found ourselves imagining what life had been like a hundred years earlier, here on D Street.

Afterward, we camped in the hills north of Virginia City where a hungry herd of cattle awakened and frightened us as they snorted and pulled at tufts of grass beside our tent. We laughed afterwards but we were terrified at the time.

The search for Rosa May was exciting and interesting for my wife and I and we loved the old world it enfolded. My wife was very helpful, often coming up with new ideas and finding documents where I had previously and thoroughly searched.

There were two questions about Rosa's life we had not found answers: 1) when did she come to Bodie, and, 2) when did she die.

Earlier in the research, I believed a deed for a house could help pin-point the years Rosa had lived in Bodie. I had gone through Mono County land records several times on my own and found nothing. However I still believed that Rosa May had owned property in Bodie. The deed that could prove so, was lost somewhere in the Bridgeport Courthouse. I was determined to find the deed.

In the meantime, I had found two important lists of early Bodie property owners. The first, was a list drawn up in 1880 when Bodie petitioned to incorporate. The second, was a list of property owners mentioned in the 1884 Bodie Fire Tax list. What is important about these lists is that they name the early Bodie red light operators.

We made a list of the early red light operators. We believed by tracing each name, we would discover who the early operators had sold out to. Hopefully, Rosa May would eventually turn up. It was a long shot but it was worth a try.

Edie and I began patiently tracing each property owner in the Bridgeport Courthouse, going down the long lists of names in the huge Grantor-Grantee Indexes. We were tracing the name "Rodriguez" when my wife came across a scribbled name which appeared to be Rosa May. It was a deed to Rosa May's house. A clerk had mistakenly filed the deed under Rosa May's first name instead of her last.

In Book 0, page 41, we found the deed. Dated June 14, 1902, it states that Rosa May purchased Lot 42 of Block 26 in the Bodie red light district for $175 from a Hugh McCaghren. Here was documented proof that Rosa May had owned land in Bodie, and proof that she was still alive in 1902.

The deed gave us one more gem: it states that Rosa May had occupied this house as a residence "upwards of ten years." This meant that Rosa May had more than likely arrived in Bodie about 1892 at the age of thirty-eight.

Bodie in the 1890's was certainly in no better economic shape than the Comstock Lode where Rosa May had worked. Bodie's days as a boom camp were twenty years past. The camp would have perished had the cyanide process not been discovered and introduced into the Bodie mining facilities. This new process of gold extraction kept the camp alive and able to support a population of a thousand to fifteen hundred. That number would dwindle to eight hundred by 1900, and would dwindle further year by year until World War I, when mining ceased in Bodie for a time.

It would appear from the deed of 1902, that Rosa May permanently arrived in Bodie around 1892, and until that time, more than likely had continued working brothels in Virginia and Carson City, and possibly Reno, which was only thirty miles from Carson. Her drifting to Bodie may not have been purely dictated by economics. At thirty-eight, after years of a precarious existence, moving from one brothel to another, perhaps Rosa May longed for stability. The fact that Ernest Marks, Rosa's lover of her earlier years, was in Bodie, certainly had some effect on her decision to go to that camp.

New Years, 1880, is the last correspondence we have between Marks and Rosa May. It is not known what happened between them. It seems that they were separated a number of years. Ernest Marks was living in Bodie as early as March, 1884.

In March, 1884, several pages of the Lundy newspaper were given to a shooting involving Ernest Marks, Charlie Jardine, and Lundy Sheriff, Kirk Steves. Lundy was a mining camp some twenty-five miles southeast of Bodie.

From the article, it seems that Marks and Jardine were friends, though Jardine was known as a Bodie bad character. Apparently, there were bad feelings between Jardine and Kirk Steves. Steves had egged Jardine into a fight. Several shots were fired by the three men, Marks being on Jardine's side. Jardine was shot in the leg. Marks and Steves escaped injury.

Ernest Marks was later arraigned in Bridgeport for the Lundy shooting. He was released and the matter was later dismissed. Jardine was later shot and killed in Bodie. Kirk Steves suffered the same fate in Aurora in 1911, by a saloon keeper. The writer of the Bridgeport *Chronicle-Union* article, claimed Steves was quarrelsome when drinking and was involved in several shooting scrapes. "Steves," the writer said, "when in liquor was continually threatening to kill someone and it is a surprise that he was not killed years ago."

The Lundy article went on to explain, that Ernest Marks worked for Morris Marks and Company, a wholesale liquor dealer in Bodie. Morris was Ernest's older brother and had left Gold Hill in 1879 when Bodie boomed and set up a permanent business there that year. Morris Marks left Bodie in the late 1880's, at which time Ernest took over his saloon which he operated until 1919 when prohibition forced Ernest out of business.

In Bodie, Rosa May lived in what was called the "lower end", or the Chinatown area. She rented the small white house on Bonanza Street which she later purchased. In 1900 there were about fifty Chinese living in Chinatown. In 1893, there were certainly more.

Fifty feet from Rosa's front door, there was a corral, a stable and a small jail. Beyond this was Main Street at the foot of Bodie Bluff where the mines were located.

By moving to Bodie, Rosa had not placed herself in entirely unfamiliar surroundings. Many of the men living in Bodie had come down from the Comstock when Virginia's mines played out. Some of these men became Bodie's principal businessmen.

Antonio Maestretti, who ran a bakery in Virginia City, was a saloon keeper in Bodie. Pete Tobin, who had tended bar in Virginia City, opened his own saloon in Bodie. Harvey Boone, another ex-Virginian, operated a general store in Bodie. Jim Cain, who had worked in the Carson wood yards, became a banker and chief businessman. Hank Blanchard had operated a freight company between Carson and Bodie, later between Bodie and Aurora. Many of Bodie's miners were also men who had worked Virginia's mines.

Mining camp people lived on the excitement and fast money of the boom camp. When one boom camp hit the skids, people moved onto the next.

It is impossible to know exactly how many prostitutes were in Bodie in the 1890's. Had the entire 1890 Census not been destroyed by fire, we could have known the number. More than likely, there were no more than a handful.

It appears that Rosa May's good friend, Emma Goldsmith, also ended up in Bodie in the 1890's. Goldsmith had operated a brothel in Carson City. She was arrested several times, once for using opium. August 18, 1900, Goldsmith was charged with the crime of insanity. She was released and eventually drank herself to death by October 13, 1900. A few brief lines in the Bridgeport *Chronicle-Union* marked her end: "Dead—Emma

Goldsmith—one of Bodie's lowest levels, died about 3 o'clock this morning."

By the turn of the century, there were 141 red light districts in the United States. By 1925, only one in Reno, Nevada. The red light districts of Minneapolis, Portland and Los Angeles would close by 1913, Denver by 1915. San Francisco's Barbary Coast, the Uptown Tenderloin, and New Orleans's Storyville would close by 1917.

The Golden Era of the American Brothel was coming to an end brought on by anti-prostitution groups, purity reform, the woman's suffrage movement, and the temperance movement. Women, the nation over, were taking an active part in ridding the family of that which had most often harmed it: alcohol, gambling, and prostitution.

The efforts of these movements were felt even in Bodie. In June, 1906, saloon keepers complained that Bodie was becoming a temperance town. July 13, 1907, Mono County Board of Supervisors passed an ordinance requiring saloon keepers to apply for liquor licenses quarterly, charging a one dollar license fee. The ordinance, aimed specifically at Bodie prostitutes, prohibited women in saloons and authorized the revocation of liquor licenses for law breakers. The ordinance was enforced January 13, 1912, when Antonio Maestretti and Ed Murphy lost their licenses for allowing women to frequent their saloons.

March 20, 1909, the Nevada legislature passed an anti-gambling amendment. In 1911 Mono County followed suit with Ordinance 113 which prohibited gambling in saloons. The ordinance forced gamblers to frequent the red district, where gambling was oddly allowed to continue. The Bridgeport *Chronicle Union* of August 19, 1911, attacked the new gambling ordinance:

Today there are as many men at work in the town of Bodie as there was a year ago. They receive the same wages as they did at that time and yet the town is dull. There has been no church revival, no man has been sent to the penitentiary for embezzlement or spending money that belonged to his creditors, yet the boys get rid of their money—and with people who pay neither taxes or license.

One year ago there were two or three houses of prostitution and about the same number of inmates. Now there are four times as many and the red lights burn till dawn. The men who were in the habit of playing a game or two of cards in a saloon now spend their money in less desirable places.

...Bodie is a mining camp. It has no theaters, parks, library or other place where a single man can spend his idle hours. For the young man the open saloon is better than the red light district and Chinatown.

Gambling behind closed doors is patronized more fully by young men than it is that in a public place, and the crooked gambler is always present in such a place. If Ordinance No. 113 has improved the moral status of Bodie (the place in Mono County at which it was aimed) the betterment is not visible ... it is a breeder of crime, compelling hypocrisy and making a bad matter worse...

Ordinance 113 was not revoked and Bodie prostitutes continued reaping its benefits.

In 1880, one third of California's population were women, a large number of these were prostitutes who had helped to settle California during the gold rush.

By 1900, there were now many respectable women, and more families. Prostitution posed a threat to these.

On April 7, 1913, after pressure from reform groups, the California legislature passed the Red Light Abatement Act. The act states that, "Every building or place used for immoral purposes is a nuisance which shall be enjoined, abated and prevented as hereinafter provided, whether the same be public or private nuisance." The new law authorized fines and/or imprisonment for the owners of such property who violated the law and, the removal and sale of all furnishings (including musical instruments) and the closing building to any occupancy for one year.

The Red Light Abatement Act was placed on the November 1914 ballot as a referendum. The people of California voted the referendum into law which became effective December 19, 1914. Many strongly opposed the law, which they considered unconstitutional. In 1917, the California Supreme Court ruled the Red Light Abatement Act was constitutional. So began the crack-down on all California red light districts.

Ironically, the strong wave of anti-prostitution sentiment

came as Rosa May neared the end of her life in Bodie, California.

We found it difficult to determine exactly when Rosa May died. Mono County death records go back as far as the 1860's. Mysteriously they were without record of Rosa May's death. Rosa had died after 1906. At that time Mono County clerks were more diligent than predecessors. There should have been a death certificate.

Evidently, the attending physician—if there had been one, did not file a death certificate. Rosa May's friends had not nor the undertaker.

Mono County health records were without history of epidemics which made it impossible to pinpoint the Bodie pneumonia epidemic which supposedly claimed Rosa's life.

After 1900, vital statistics for every county in California were sent to Sacramento and recorded by the Bureau of Vital Statistics. I contacted the Bureau and had them search their records between 1900-18 for a death of Rosa May. They found nothing.

Finally, I searched through every newspaper published in the Bodie region between 1900-18 in hopes of finding a mention of Rosa's death. These newspapers included: the Bridgeport *Chronicle-Union*, Hawthorne's, *Walker Lake Bulletin*; the *Aurora Borealis*, Mina, Nevada's, *Western Nevada Miner* and the few surviving issues of the Bodie *Miner*.

While searching the November 17, 1906 issue of the Bridgeport *Chronicle-Union*, I thought I had finally found what I was looking for. Under "Bodie Items" there were these brief lines:

A woman resident of Chinatown died Sunday evening at 8 o'clock coroner's inquest was held Monday by Judge Moyle and the jury failed to agree as to the cause of her death. On Tuesday a postmortem examination revealed the fact that alcoholism was the cause of her death. The body was buried in Potter's field Tuesday by friends.

The item had all the pertinent facts: Chinatown woman, obviously a prostitute, dies of alcoholism, is buried by friends in Potter's field, the outcast cemetery.

In the Bridgeport Courthouse I searched for the coroner's

inquest, to discover whether or not the woman was in fact Rosa May. I did not find the inquest. I later learned a Molly Piantoni appeared on the 1905-06 delinquent tax list. She had owned lots 39 and 40 of Block 26 in the red light. It would seem from this information, that Molly Piantoni was the prostitute who had died of alcoholism. Several things pointed to this:

In his book, *Mining Camp Days*, Emil Billeb mentions that Rosa May, along with Big Bonanza, Big Nell and Bull Con Josey, were the Bodie prostitutes when Billeb arrived in 1908 to take over management of the Bodie and Benton railroad. Emil Billeb is dead, but those who knew him, say he had a marvelous memory. Billeb's information coincides with that of Sadie Cain and Anna McKenzie who saw Rosa May as late as 1910.

I believe Rosa May died between November, 1911 and November, 1912. She is listed in the 1910 federal census and was alive at that time. Rosa May's property appeared on the 1912-13 Mono County delinquent tax list. Her property tax became delinquent November, 1912. The property went up for tax sale on June, 1913 and was assessed at a value of $210, $35 more than the 1902 purchase price.

In 1918, Rosa's property was sold to the State of California. Her house and other red light and Chinatown buildings were torn down by 1919.

The Bodie *Miner* more than likely mentioned Rosa's death. Unfortunately I was unable to find the particular issue.

The Bridgeport *Chronicle-Union* was an extremely conservative paper. Yet, in the past it had carried the deaths of prostitutes, even squaws, then considered lower than prostitutes. But the *Chronicle-Union* did not mention Rosa May's death. One wonders why.

A handful of Bodie women had managed to force men to bury Rosa outside the fence. But the *Chronicle Union*—always hard up for news gave Rosa May the final humiliating blow by not mentioning her death.

The last interesting pieces of information come from two old timers, Guy McInnis and Herb DeChambeau, who lived in Bodie before and after the turn of the century.

Throughout my research, I was often told that Guy

McInnis was the oldest survivor of Bodie's earlier days. I had written him several times. Each time my letter was returned with a polite note that said Mr. McInnis was quite elderly, nearly blind, and of no help to me besides. But I didn't believe that and managed to get Guy's phone number from a daughter-in-law. Guy now lived in Las Vegas; I called him.

I introduced myself and asked Guy about turn of the century Bodie and Rosa May. I soon learned Guy knew more than he thought he knew. I persuaded him to allow me to interview him.

Several days later my wife and I drove two hundred and fifty miles to Las Vegas. We stayed the night in Vegas before interviewing Guy the next morning. During the night I became very sick for no apparent reason. The next morning we had an awful time finding Guy's house. After an hour's search, we found it, a green stucco house in a middle-class neighborhood whose streets were scrambled like a maze.

Guy McInnis, born in 1882, was ninety-five. He was pale and silver haired. He had a sharp mind and a good memory but unfortunately his eyes were very bad and he was unable to identify pictures of Bodie. As I spoke with him he tapped his fingers nervously on his rocking chair and breathed heavily. He was polite and tried hard to remember things I asked about. Guy wanted to know what I would do with the information, so I told him.

As a young man, he had worked as a clerk in Cecil Burkham's general store. Burkham's carried everything, groceries, candy, hardware, dry goods, Christmas things and fruits in season.

The telephone was brought to Bodie around 1900. The red light women would phone Burkham, place their orders and Guy would deliver them. The red light women seldom came uptown. He had heard that the prostitutes sometimes frequented the saloons at night, but Guy could not recall them doing so.

It was on his deliveries to the red light district that Guy saw Rosa May a few times. He says that Rosa was, "a very quiet woman...not very handsome, stout as far as I remember, short and stout. Must have been in her forties. Don't remember what color hair she had. It was common knowledge in Bodie that Marks lived down there with her."

When I asked Guy how the townspeople felt about that, Guy said, "They didn't pay any attention to it as far as I know."

"Marks", he said, "outside of running his saloon didn't mix with society. He was bummed up with rheumatism. I know he walked with a cane. Now Neuman Tobias, his bartender, was something like Marks himself. Fifty years of age or more, quiet sort of man. He was a Jew too."

As far as Guy knew, Rosa had continued in prostitution as long as Marks lived with her. He insisted that Rosa was never a madam.

There were about four houses of prostitution in Bodie at the time. Emma Goldsmith's place was just north of Jim Cain's bank, near the corner of King and Main Street, back a ways and facing main.

Guy could not remember Rosa's death nor the pneumonia epidemic which supposedly took her life. He did say there was a year when the "grip" was real bad.

"That must have been a curious crowd up there that made them dig her grave outside," Guy said. "It's just like the Lord said, "Let ye without sin cast the first stone. I can't see why they had to bury her there. She didn't contaminate the ground a' tall."

That was all Guy could remember. He wished he could remember more and apologized for not being able to. I told him he had helped us an awful lot. He carefully walked us out to our car, this kind old man who was nearly blind. He seemed so lonely as we left him and he stood and watched our car as we drove away. He seemed to me to be like a willow that had bent so much in so many years that he was simply tired of bending. Guy McInnis died two weeks later.

Herb DeChambeau was born in the Bodie area in 1888. He was 88 when we interviewed him in San Diego. He had lived a fascinating full life of which he spoke excitedly. He had driven hay teams and stages, broke horses and hiked up mountains carrying ninety pounds of mail. He had been a cowboy, a miner, and millman in Bodie's Standard Mill. He had joined up as a bugler in the Spanish American War, and sought excitement as a soldier, volunteering for the Canadian Army in 1916. He had had a good life and talked of it with zest and humor in a raspy voice as he stretched himself on the bed where he spent most of his time. The three of us sipped whisky and soda which Herb had eagerly and generously poured. Laid up like he was, the whisky seemed to help Herb remember the days when he lived in Bodie shortly before the camp's demise.

Herb told us of Bodie's big saloons, how the sawdust covered the floors and a beer cost ten cents a mug, five for a Pony schooner, how all the saloon keepers laid out meat, cheese and bread on the counter for the popular free lunches. He told us about Marks' saloon, how Marks, like Seller another saloon keeper, was very stand-offish. Marks was about 57, medium build mustached and gray haired.

Herb lived in Bodie in 1898 and 99, and 1908 up through the fall of 1911. He and the "boys" had often frequented the Bodie red light, or Angel's roost" as he called it. It was there in the Bodie red light between 1908 and 1911 that Herb met Rosa May, who was about fifty, and too old for prostitution, he claims. She had three or four girls working for her. A beer went for two bits— a quarter—and two dollars paid for one of Rosie's girls in the backroom.

Marks lived "down there" with Rosa and everyone knew about it. Marks, however, never talked about Rosa.

It is interesting that Herb Dechambeau remembered Rosa as a madam. The Bridgeport *Chronicle-Union* carried these lines December, 1909:

The tent house in which Rosie and her girls are living caught on fire last Sunday. One end of the tent was burned out and most of their clothing burnt It is not known how the fire started.

This fire took place in Masonic, a gold camp fifteen miles from Bodie which then had a population of about five hundred lonely, sex starved men. Very likely, the Rosie mentioned was Rosa May who apparently, had employed several girls.

Several things account for this: One, Rosa was no longer the good looking woman of earlier years.

Secondly, the recent mining boom in Masonic and Lucky Boy had increased Mono County population by eight hundred, many of these, single men employed in mines. There was, therefore, more money to be made from prostitution.

Third, the recent banning of saloon gambling had increased the popularity of the red light district where men could still gamble, adding to prostitution's profits. Certainly, these factors must have encouraged Rosa May to bring in younger prostitutes from the outside.

From this information, it appears that Rosa May was a madam for a short time toward the end of her life.

Chapter 14

Greater love hath no man than this, that a man lay down his life for his friends. John 15:13

It was early morning and very cold. A thin sheet of frost lay on our tent, and when we exhaled a stream of white vapor blew from our mouths. The sun's yellow rays lit up part of the valley but its warmth had not reached us yet as the campground lay in the cold dark shadow of Bodie Bluff. I was hoping the sun would rise quickly over the mountain but I knew it would take time.

I pumped the Coleman stove vigorously, then turned the black knob that released the gas fumes into the burner. The fumes, white from the cold, sputtered out the black holes. I struck a match and the fumes puffed into a greenish-blue flame. Fire at last. I warmed my cold hands over the flames.

Nearby there is a spring that runs year round. I filled the copper-bottomed saucepan with cold spring water, heated it on the Coleman and poured the steaming water into two cups with instant hot chocolate. I woke my wife and gave her the hot chocolate and we talked about how cold it was.

It was September again high in the Bodie Hills. We were the only campers foolish or poor enough to brave the cold, Bodie night in a nylon tent.

When we finished the hot chocolate, we put our wool-knit caps on and bundled ourselves in sweaters and jackets. I grabbed the hand-axe and photos. My wife brought the camera, and Harvey, our Springer Spaniel, ran ahead as we walked around the ghost town, south to the cemetery. This early in the morning, no one would disturb us.

Late in the afternoon of the previous day, my wife and I had been working in the cemetery, searching for Rosa's actual grave which had been lost over the years. The sky grew somber with brooding, black clouds and it began to rain. I didn't want the photos to get wet so we took shelter in the nearby morgue.

184

I was disturbed that afternoon by our repeated bad luck which seemed to always overtake us in Bodie. Our car, which ran well over mountains and deserts, suddenly developed mechanical problems in Bodie, faulty fuel pumps, flat tires, sudden shortages of gas and oil, and finally, a thrown rod. Always in Bodie, nowhere else.

It seemed to us that something wanted to frustrate or hamper our progress. These feelings became more eerie when I recalled how on several occasions, I had felt a dark, oppressive force while standing beside Rosa's grave. Our repeated bad luck in Bodie and this dark feeling caused me to secretly believe that this something, whatever it was, did not want Rosa May's story told. And now the rain, when we were so close to locating Rosa's grave.

But on this morning, the sky was clear and there were no signs of rain. I prayed that we would have good luck with our search.

We climbed the sagebrush slopes to the outcast cemetery where I left my wife while Harvey and I continued up the hill, through the regular cemetery, to the place where Burton Frasher shot his 1927 photos. These were the only early photos of Bodie cemetery showing Rosa's picket fence just outside the cemetery. Positioning myself at the point where Frasher had taken his photos, I would try again to pinpoint Rosa's grave by comparing landmarks in the cemetery with landmarks in the town beyond.

I was now about two hundred yards from my wife. "Walk that way," I yelled, and pointed which direction. "Keep going." I looked at the photos again. "Now come forward. More. More. That's right." I studied the photos once again. "Now a little to your left. All right. Stay there, I think that's it."

I ran down through the cemetery, dodging graves and sagebrush to my wife. Sure enough, where she stood, there was a small mound of dirt covered by sagebrush, the trunk of which, was as thick as my forearm. I grabbed the hand-axe and chopped the brush away. The small mound was obviously the grave of a tiny woman. My wife and I smiled. I raised my arms up. "This is it. This is her grave," and we were so happy to have found it.

Louis Serventi's concrete marker stood about one hundred and fifty feet northwest of Rosa's actual grave. Though Serventi had unknowingly misplaced his marker, it was his gravestone that had made me curious. I was grateful. Had he not made the marker, I likely would have never become interested in Rosa May's story.

It had all begun here in the outcast cemetery, and it seemed fitting it should end here. We gathered large stones and piled them on the tiny mound so Rosa's grave would not be lost again.

As I stood beside Rosa's grave, I felt great satisfaction for having begun the search and for having stuck with it for as long as it had taken. We had gone through every courthouse record, police record, newspaper, census; read every book and article; and interviewed many people seeking information about Rosa May. Now the work was done. There was nothing more to do. We were relieved.

It was here in the mining camp of Bodie, in this green mountain valley below barren bluffs, that Rosa Elizabeth White—who later called herself, Rosa May, had died in the winter of 1911-1912 at the age of fifty-seven, having spent forty-one years of her life as a prostitute. They had dragged her coffin by sled up the snowy slopes and buried her here in the outcast cemetery, some hundred feet outside the fence. A picket fence was placed around her grave which was eventually destroyed by weather or stolen. No stone was placed on her grave. No newspaper had mourned her passing. No document had marked her end. It was if Rosa May had never lived. But she had, and there were reasons she had lived as she had.

Born in 1855, a daughter of Irish immigrants, Rosa May was a wonderfully warm, inquisitive child who had the misfortune of having been born into a terribly suppressive, unstable home. Misunderstanding and the ill treatment by her parents, bred in Rosa feelings of worthlessness and guilt which dominated and motivated her life. Due to this ill treatment, she would never lead a happy, normal life.

In 1871, at the age of sixteen, Rosa ran away from her home in Pennsylvania. She drifted to New York City where she fell in with a hard crowd of young men and women as badly damaged as herself. Soon she was prostituting to survive, a choice she made freely, aware of what she was doing. In prostitution, she found a place to belong among other homeless souls like herself. She drifted in a bizarre, lonely world of superficial relationships—a life without bottom, where men and women used each other.

In 1871, having heard of the good money to be made in mining camps, Rosa May, like thousands of eastern prostitutes, went west. She worked the Colorado and Idaho mining camp brothels for two years. In 1873, she moved on to Virginia City, Nevada, just in time for the fantastic boom of 1874. She worked the Virginia City, Carson City and Reno circuit of whorehouses for the next twenty years.

She eventually drifted to Bodie in the early 1890's where she lived until her death in 1911-12. In the few years before her death, she may have earned her living as a madam. However the majority of evidence leads one to believe she was a prostitute to the end.

About 1877, she met Ernest Marks in Virginia City. Rosa and Marks fell in love and remained lovers while Rosa worked as a prostitute. In the early 1880's it appears they separated, Marks moving on to Bodie with his brother Morris. Their relationship resumed when Rosa came to Bodie about 1893.

From 1893 until her death, Rosa and Marks had a steady relationship. Marks lived with her in the red light district as Rosa May continued in prostitution. Rosa May was loyal and tenacious and stayed with Marks, although he was unstable, ill-tempered and violent.

After Rosa May's death, in spite of the years they had spent together, Marks never placed a fitting monument on her grave. He took up with other Bodie prostitutes who robbed and left him. He spent his last years crippled by arthritis. He was often seen hobbling along the boardwalks, leaning on his ever present cane.

In 1919 prohibition drove Marks out of the saloon business. He lived in his saloon alone, supported by relatives in the east, until his death in 1928. Though legend claims he was buried beside Rosa, his death certificate states that he was buried in the Odd Fellows cemetery, within the fence. His grave remains unmarked.

There was little evidence Rosa May died while nursing miners during one of Bodie's pneumonia epidemics. Newspapers, always looking for interesting items, carried no stories of the supposed epidemic. County health records were poorly kept and could not substantiate the epidemic. Memories of old timers were void of such a recollection.

Despite this, old timers persistently remembered Rosa May as a "good hearted" woman who helped the poor whenever she could. A graphoanalysis of her handwriting substantiates this claim: Rosa May was a woman who could be easily tempted to sacrifice herself for others.

How then, had Rosa died? The epidemic Ella Cain wrote of may have actually been three or four men who came down with pneumonia. Perhaps Rosa May, known for her good heart, generous by nature, had gone to these men—most likely neighbors, had nursed them and perished in the process. There was nothing, really, to prove she had. Then again, there was nothing to prove she hadn't.

Rosa May was an ordinary mining camp prostitute and her life followed the general pattern of such women. A confused young girl, emotionally damaged, without ambition or hope, she had gone into prostitution. There she found easy money and others like herself. With youth and beauty on her side, prostitution was profitable and more bearable. But with the passing years, the grueling life eventually robbed Rosa of her beauty. Profits dwindled, prostitution became a harder way of life. Many prostitutes in the declining years had killed themselves. Rosa May had not. She had gone into the life freely. Loyal and tenacious, she stuck it out until the end.

Chapter 15

We dig four holes, one at each corner of Rosa's grave. My wife and I and a young park ranger lift the fence posts into the four holes. With my shovel, I bury the posts with dirt and rock. The fence is a replica of the picket fence torn from her grave. I used old weathered lumber to give it an aged look. Now that the fence is in place, I take hold of it with my hand and give it a shake. Strong enough. I hope it will survive the hard Bodie winters and the pack rat instincts of curious visitors.

It's a hot August day in Bodie. I wipe the sweat from my forehead with my open hand. I motion to my wife for the canteen. She hands it to me. I take a long swallow of the good, sweet Bodie spring water.

The sky is very blue. Huge cotton ball clouds, like great white birds, hover in the sky. Every time we've come to this country we've found it more difficult to go back to the smoggy skies and rat race in Southern California.

Looking down the slopes from Rosa's grave you can see it all. It's pretty much the same as the first time I came to Bodie. The weathered, tobacco colored buildings stand like a ruin in the green fields. Visitors walk the fields and dirt streets. Grownups and children on tiptoes, hands on windowsills, peak inside the old buildings. They are looking for the ancient people who lived here. They peek through windows as if hoping to look through time and see, feel and hear how it was when Bodie was the roaring gold mining camp that became legend. But the ancient people they seek are dead and gone. The curious visitors find only those discarded things that couldn't find room in the cramped wagons and trucks when families pulled out of Bodie after the mines closed.

Through the windows they see stained mattresses, broken chairs, dusty chest-of-drawers, a wood burning stove, faded newspapers and such. The imaginations of these curious souls is stirred. They would love to see Bodie alive again. But they will have to settle for this ghost town, with its memories and fading stories.

Cars, trucks and campers jostle to and fro over the bone-white, dirt road below the cemetery. The kicked-up dust floats on the wind in a cloud. Some visitors are on their way out, back to the highway. Others are arriving, slowly rocking toward the large parking lot a quarter mile from the cemetery. In the parking lot, moms and dads, kids and grandparents, pile out for their first glimpse of a real ghost town.

Casually dressed in jeans, shorts and T-shirts, visitors walk the worn paths of the Bodie cemetery. With cameras about their necks, they speak excitedly of the strange wooden planks used to mark the graves, now split and faded with the years. Here, wooden fences are toppled over, graves are overrun with sagebrush, sturdy stone markers have names and dates neatly carved. The visitors count the life spans on their fingers, seeking the earliest death or the oldest human being. Many are touched by the number of children buried in the Bodie Cemetery.

Here, are buried the many men who died in the mines during Bodie's fifty year life. Some were blown up through a negligent use of dynamite. Some fell hundreds of feet down dark mine shafts. Others were victims of heat exhaustion, cave-ins, runaway ore cars. These men had gambled their lives in the mines and they had lost their bets.

In the far southwest corner of the cemetery, visitors find a strong black iron fence surrounding an unmarked grave. This is the grave of Lottie Johl, the prostitute who married Eli Johl, the butcher. Lottie died November 7, 1899, after taking a prescription that was accidentally filled with poison. She was forty-four and had come a long way from her home in Iowa to die in this rugged mining camp. Eli fought hard to have Lottie buried inside the cemetery. Some townspeople were opposed. But Lottie was no longer a prostitute Eli raged. Lottie was his wife and she would be buried inside the cemetery.

Eli won his fight. The townspeople grudgingly allowed Lottie burial inside the fence-but only in the most remote part of the cemetery, farthest from the entrance, here in the southwest corner.

And there beside Rosa May's white marker a man and wife and their ten year old daughter act out a scene I've witnessed several times. The husband and wife hold hands as they stand before Rosa's marker. They study the childlike letters. They notice that there are no dates nor place of birth. The paint has been blasted from the stone by hard weather.

"This is the woman we learned about in the museum" the husband says.

"The red light woman," the wife asks.

"Uh-huh."

"What's a red light woman, Dad?"

"Oh,…that means she was…a prostitute."

"A what?"

"Never mind Kate. You'll learn about those things soon enough," her mother says.

"Dad, c'mon. What was she?"

"She was a woman who probably had a hard life."

"Oh." The girl ponders her father's words. She spots a cluster of wild daisies near Rosa's grave. She kneels and tenderly pulls them from the earth. She lays them at the foot of Rosa's marker.

"There," she says, with obvious satisfaction.

The wife turns, and looks down at the ghost town and the barren hills beyond. "How could any woman live in a place like this?"

"I don't know."

The man and his wife turn from Rosa May's grave and begin walking down the hill to the road that leads back to their car. The girl remains beside Rosa's marker, thinking about Rosa May and what she was. A strange loneliness she has never felt surrounds her.

"Katie, c'mon," her father calls. The girl runs down the hill dodging the clumps of sagebrush. Reaching her parents she takes hold of her father's hand. She leans close to him and whispers, "You'll tell me what she was later, won't you?" The father looks at his daughter and smiles. He remembers how curious he was.

"Katie, like Mom says, you're too young to know about

some things. I know you don't understand this. We're just thinking of you. When you're older, if you still want to know, I'll tell you."

Katie's face crumples.

"Oh, all right," she moans. Her father smiles. He wraps his arms around his two favorite girls and pulls them close. "I love you," he says.

He had no beauty or majesty to attract us to him, nothing in his appearance that we should desire him.

He was despised and rejected by men, a man of sorrows, and familiar with suffering.

Like one from whom men hide their faces he was despised, and we esteemed him not.

Surely he took up our infirmities and carried our sorrows, yet we considered him stricken by God, smitten by him, and afflicted.

But he was pierced for our transgressions, he was crushed for our iniquities; the punishment that brought us peace was upon him, and by his wounds we are healed.

Isaiah 53: 2-5